Tracing Your Ancestors
Using the UK
Historical Timeline

Tracing Your Ancestors Using the UK Historical Timeline

A Guide for Family Historians

Angela Smith and Neil Bertram

Pen & Sword
FAMILY HISTORY

First published in Great Britain in 2021 and reprinted in 2022 and
2023 by
Pen & Sword Family History
An imprint of
Pen & Sword Books Ltd
Yorkshire – Philadelphia

ISBN 978 1 39900 332 2

Typeset by Mac Style
Printed in the UK on paper from a sustainable source by
CPI Group (UK) Ltd, Croydon, CR0 4YY

Pen & Sword Books Limited incorporates the imprints of Atlas,
Archaeology, Aviation, Discovery, Family History, Fiction, History,
Maritime, Military, Military Classics, Politics, Select, Transport,
True Crime, Air World, Frontline Publishing, Leo Cooper, Remember
When, Seaforth Publishing, The Praetorian Press, Wharncliffe
Local History, Wharncliffe Transport, Wharncliffe True Crime
and White Owl.

For a complete list of Pen & Sword titles please contact

PEN & SWORD BOOKS LIMITED
47 Church Street, Barnsley, South Yorkshire, S70 2AS, England
E-mail: enquiries@pen-and-sword.co.uk
Website: www.pen-and-sword.co.uk

Or

PEN AND SWORD BOOKS
1950 Lawrence Rd, Havertown, PA 19083, USA
E-mail: Uspen-and-sword@casematepublishers.com
Website: www.penandswordbooks.com

*Dedicated to our families who we have
bored to death with family history!
Our grateful thanks to Debbie, Judith, Allan
and other friends and family who have kindly
read through earlier drafts of this book and
offered their comments.*

Contents

Introduction

Once upon a time, many years ago…well that's just the whole point; 'many years ago' – just who can remember all those dates? Don't answer that – some of us have to have them written down…

So, this handbook has been compiled as a tool for the family historian and in particular those new to genealogy or whose knowledge (or memory) of dates is shaky. It is not meant to be an exhaustive list of historical events. Rather, this timeline offers a guide for family historians to refer to and to help set dates into a wider historical context. It is selective; we have included items that we think are particularly important for family historians to know but there are many more that have not been cited. We have, for example, numerous references to the various taxes that have been imposed down the centuries since the paper trail for their collection might name your ancestor. There are many additional taxes that could be included – a tax on wallpaper for example in 1712 and another on the use of bricks in 1784, for which some records survive.

The main column on each page lists events pertinent to family historians where there may be some traceable record. Items in italics may not yield any records but are of interest to family historians. Some items only have the briefest of descriptions but the reader should be able to easily find more detailed information on events or source records by using the phrases in an internet search engine. Inclusion (or not) does not necessarily imply that some sort of traceable record is available.

Two smaller columns may be found on the edge of each page. These include a column listing English monarchs and prime ministers: 'Monarchy, State and Church'. The reader will find further information of a more general nature in the adjacent column which will hopefully offer some historical context: 'Socio-cultural'.

We have indicated, in a few places, if original records are kept in The National Archives (TNA), in local record offices (LROs) or in specialist niche repositories like the Imperial War Museum. We have avoided giving too many specific details as these can be easily found by the reader using keywords in an internet search engine. An excellent place to start is TNA Discovery which holds more than 32 million descriptions of records held by them and more than 2,500 archives across the country:

https://discovery.nationalarchives.gov.uk. A few other websites are given where we are reasonably certain the web address will not change. For a virtual reference library of genealogical information, with particular relevance to the UK and Ireland, see: www.genuki.org.uk.

All population numbers are approximate – averaged from several sources as nobody seems to agree! Dates are as accurate as humanly possible; legislation can be quoted as the date it was passed or date it was enacted.

The future looks bright for Family Historians! More and more records are being made available all the time; especially at the moment as records for workers across many diverse trades are being released for general viewing. Keep searching and if they are not there today they just maybe tomorrow.

We really do hope you find the information useful in some way. Even if you find one nugget of information that prompts you to search new areas for your ancestors or offers some context in which to place their situation. Happy searching!

About the Authors

Angela has a PhD in Combined Historical Studies (Warburg Institute, London) and is a freelance lecturer for the Arts Society. She and her husband Adrian live in Somerset. Nearly 45 years ago Angela could be found walking to school with Neil. Now both have been reunited through their love of digging up the past.

Neil has worked in publishing, primarily design and editing. Was a London Taxi (Black Cabs) driver for ten years. Worked on research and volunteer/events coordinator for Boathouse 4 in Portsmouth Historic Dockyard. Neil gained BA (Hons) in History as a mature student. He currently works in adult social care.

Abbreviations

BL	British Library
DNB	Dictionary of National Biography
EU	European Union
FFHS	Federation of Family History Societies
GRO	General Register Office for England and Wales
HMC	Historic Manuscripts Commission
HMSO	Her Majesty's Stationery Office
JRL	John Rylands Library
LMA	London Metropolitan Archives
LRO	Local Record Office/Archive
LSE	London School of Economics
NAI	National Archives of Ireland
NRA	National Register of Archives
NRAS	National Register of Archives of Scotland
NRS	National Records of Scotland
ONS	Office for National Statistics
OPCS	Office of Population Censuses and Surveys
OPSI	Office of Public Sector Information
PRO	Public Record Office, formerly in Chancery Lane, now part of TNA
PRONI	Public Record Office of Northern Ireland
SPCK	Society for the Promotion of Christian Knowledge
TNA	The National Archives
VCH	Victoria County History

Chapter One

1000s

	Socio-Cultural	Monarchy, State and Church

1066

After his conquest of England, William the Conqueror (William I) re-distributed land, granting tracts across England to his Norman followers and also the church.

1067

William I issued the first charter to the City of London

Norman barons often adopted the name of their lands in England (and Normandy) as surnames.

1070s

The Bayeux Tapestry, the *Gesta Guillelmi II Ducis Normannorum* and the *Historia Ecclesiastica*, provide the names of 15 'proven companions' of William the Conqueror at Hastings.

1086

The Doomsday Survey was collated. It was the earliest systematic survey of land ownership in England and gives details of land owners and the status of individual taxpayers. It is available online and in print.

Socio-Cultural	Monarchy, State and Church
1066 Feudalism took hold after the Norman Conquest Extensive programme of castle building	**1066** Battle of Hastings **1066 (to 1154)** House of Normandy **1066 (to 1087)** **William (I) the Conqueror**
	1070s (to c1220) Growth of monasticism
1079 The Isle of Man was under rule by the Norse	**1077** First Cluniac priory at Lewes
	1087 (to 1100) **William (II) Rufus**

Socio-Cultural Timeline	Monarchy, State and Church

1093

Norman settlement of Pembrokeshire

1094
Welsh revolt against the Normans

1096 (to 1099)

First Crusade

Chapter Two

1100s

	Socio-Cultural Timeline	Monarchy, State and Church
	1100 Population 2 million	**1100 (to 1135)** **Henry I**
		1106 Augustinian (black) canons established their first abbey near Colchester
	1119 Knights Templar founded	
		1124 (to 1153) **King David I** (reunited Scotland)
		1128 First Cistercian abbey founded at Waverley
		c1130 The Gilbertines founded
	1135 Outbursts of anti-Semitic violence	**1135 (to 1154)** **Stephen**
		1136 Welsh defeat Normans at Crug Mawr

1100s

The guild system began to develop as craftsmen sought to protect trade, set prices and offer apprenticeships.

Large numbers of farmers from the Low Countries settled in the area of The Wash, East Anglia.

1120

White Ship sank off Normandy coast with a loss of 300 including the only legitimate son of King Henry I of England.

1127

The first documented evidence for heraldry occured when Geoffrey Plantagenet was knighted. Thereafter the art of heraldry began to develop.

1130

A series of financial records kept by the Exchequer for the Crown known as Pipe Rolls were introduced. They record Exchequer payments and names of tenants.

Surnames began to be used more widely by landowners to assert their rights to hereditary property.

Socio-Cultural Timeline	Monarchy, State and Church	

1139 (to 1149)

Civil War over succession rights between Stephen and Matilda. The period was later named The Anarchy by Victorian historians.

1143
The first Premonstratensian house in England

1144 (to 1149)

Second Crusade

1154 (to 1399)
House of Plantagenet

1154 (to 1189)
Henry II

1155

The weavers were granted a royal charter making them the oldest livery company in London.

1161–2

The Danegeld tax, first raised in 991 to pay off Viking raiders, was finally abolished.

1167

Oxford University began to grow swiftly. Names and place of birth of alumni have been published in printed form as well as online.

1170
Population of London was greater than 30,000

1170
Murder of Thomas Becket, canonised in 1173

1170s

Anglo-Norman nobles were permitted to take lands in Ireland.

1171
High Kingship in
Ireland ended (when
Normans invaded)

1185

Henry II ordered an enquiry into the
assets and status of widows and wards in
estates held directly of the Crown *Rotuli
de Dominabus et Pueris et Puellis de XII
Comitatibus* (rolls concerning demesnes,
boys and girls from 12 counties),
published in book form.

1185
Lincoln Cathedral
was partially
destroyed by an
earthquake

The earliest
recorded windmill
in England was
built at Weedley in
Yorkshire

The Templars similarly enquired into the
extent and value of landed holdings in a
number of English counties, of widows
and recently-deceased tenants in chief in
Rotuli de Dominabus which gives ages and
number of children.

1187

The judgments pertaining to land
ownership called Feet of Fines began,
and are a source for surnames.

1188

The travels of Gerald of Wales, whose
notes have been published, offer detailed
observations on the Welsh landscape and
life.

Saladin Tithe levied in England to
provide funds for the Third Crusade.

1189 (to 1192)

Third Crusade

1189 and 1190
Massacres of Jews
in London and York

1189 (to 1199)
Richard I
(The Lionheart)

Socio-Cultural Timeline	Monarchy, State and Church

1192
Carlisle comes
under English rule

1194

Justices presided over legal cases in courts across England from the early 1100s but the earliest surviving Eyre Roll dates from 1194. (TNA)

1195 (to 1833)

Legal records survive from the late 12th century. Some have been published. These include the Curia Regis rolls which record the business of the court held before the king's justiciars and the Assize Rolls which record dealings of courts at a local level. (TNA)

1198 (to 1292)

A list of feudal landholdings was made. Known as the *Liber Feodorum*, it is available online and in print.

1199 (to 1216)
John

1199 (to 1517)

Charter Rolls began recording royal grants issued by the Chancery. (TNA)

Chapter Three

1200s

	Socio-Cultural Timeline	Monarchy, State and Church

Early 1200s

Manorial records recording administrative details of estates began. Their use is widespread by the end of the century.

1200
Population
3.5 million

1200s

The first monumental brasses are used in English churches to commemorate the dead.

1202

The Patent Rolls start which contain a record of royal correspondence (letters patent). They are a useful source for tracing individuals in the Middle Ages.

1202 (to 1204)
Fourth Crusade

1204

Close Rolls began which recorded grants made by the monarch to individuals and groups. (TNA)

1204
King John imposed English laws, concerning property and inheritance on the Irish

1209

Beginnings of Cambridge University. Names of alumni have been published.

Normandy incorporated into France. Jersey, Alderney and Guernsey aligned themselves with England

1210
All Jewish householders in England were imprisoned in Bristol

Socio-Cultural Timeline	Monarchy, State and Church
1213 (to 1221) Fifth Crusade	**1214** Following the Battle of Bouvines, King John was forced to surrender most of his continental lands to the French
	1215 Magna Carta
	1216 (to 1272) Henry III
	1220 (until 1538) Thomas Becket's shrine in Canterbury Cathedral began to draw thousands of pilgrims
	1221 Dominicans (black friars) arrived in England
	1224 Franciscans (grey friars) arrived in England
1228 (to 1229) Sixth Crusade	
1230s-1240s Oxford and Cambridge Universities granted Royal Charters	**1236** Commons Act allowed manorial lords to enclose common land for their own use
1242 Gunpowder introduced into Europe	

1226 (to 1426)

Liberate Rolls began recording payments made by the Crown to various individuals associated with the (very large) royal household, such as stipends and pensions. The rolls offer particularly detailed information for the mid 13th century. (TNA)

c1240 (to 1660)

The earliest Inquisitions Post Mortem (escheats) date from this period. They are useful for tracing inheritance of property, family descents and alliances, especially between 1270 and 1350. Many IPMs have been published.

1244

The earliest surviving records of sessions of Crown pleas at the Tower of London overseen by Justices Itinerant. The translated records of this eyre are available online.

1248 (to 1254)
Seventh Crusade

c.1250

First map of the British Isles drawn by Matthew Paris. (BL)

1254

An assessment of the clergy was undertaken for taxation purposes. Returns for eight dioceses survive: Bangor, Durham, Ely, Lincoln, Llandaff, London, Norwich and St Asaph.

1255 (until 1280)

Enquiries into the rights of the Crown over land and property were conducted and recorded in the Hundred Rolls (named after the county divisions called hundreds by which most returns were recorded). They were published as *Rotuli Hundredorum.*

1259
Normandy surrendered to France

Socio-Cultural Timeline	Monarchy, State and Church
	1264 Battle of Lewes brought Simon de Montfort to power as the 'uncrowned King of England'
	1264 (to 1267) Civil War
	1265 De Montfort's Parliament called in opposition to Henry III De Montfort killed at the Battle of Evesham
1267 (to 1272) Eighth Crusade	**1266** Norwegians ceded the Isle of Man to Scotland
1271 Purported arrival of Marco Polo to China	
1271 (to 1272) Ninth Crusade	**1272 (to 1307)** Edward I
1275 An earthquake was felt across England and destroyed many churches	
1277 (to 1296) New towns, Flint and Harlech, were planted adjacent to Edward I's castles in North Wales	

1266

The earliest freemen rolls date to the mid 13th century, with the first admission to the City of Exeter dating to 1266. The Exeter Rolls are almost continuous from 1286 to the present.

1272

The Husting Rolls (court records for the City of London) survive almost complete from this date.

Some of the earliest court rolls, including those for the Duchy of Lancaster, date from c1272; also Fine Rolls, which record payments to the Crown for grants and privileges.

Later 1200s

Parliamentary statute brought change to the feudal system of land ownership.

1278

Hundreds of Jews in England imprisoned on coin clipping charges. Almost 300 were executed in London.

1279–80

The surviving returns in the Hundred Rolls for these years are particularly detailed but cover only 12 counties.

1285

Statute of Winchester. Parish Constables were organized to question strangers and to patrol towns and town walls at night in an effort to maintain peace. In addition every man was required to serve the king in the event of a rebellion or a foreign invasion.

1288 (to 1292)

The Pope permitted Edward I one-tenth of the ecclesiastical income of England and Wales to pay for a crusade. A survey (digitized and available online) was made called

Socio-Cultural Timeline	Monarchy, State and Church
	1279 The Statute of Mortmain enacted to prevent land being given to the Church without royal licence
	1283 Wales came under English control
1286-7 A series of massive storms alter parts of the coastline in the south and east of England prompting the decline of Dunwich, one of England's largest towns and destroying Old Winchelsea	**1285** The Statute of Westminster formalised the system of entail
	1288 Piepowder Courts set up to try offenders at local fairs and markets

Socio-Cultural Timeline	Monarchy, State and Church

the *Taxatio Ecclesiastica* which lists 8,500 churches and chapels across the country.

1290

1290
Statutes of *Quia Emptores* and *Quo Warranto* were designed to address land ownership disputes resulting from the decline of feudalism

Records of the Mayor's Court for the City of London survive from 1290.

Edward I's Edict of Expulsion effectively expelled all Jews from England, around 16,000 left the country.

1290 (to 1334)

1294
French raids on Guernsey left many dead

Lay Subsidy Rolls began recording the taxes imposed on the laity (commoners). The rolls are a very important source for the genealogist with names recorded. The original Lay Subsidy Rolls are in the TNA, though many have been published.

1295
First legally elected legislature; the Model Parliament

1296 (to 1357)
War of Scottish Independence

Chapter Four

1300s

	Socio-Cultural Timeline		Monarchy, State and Church

1300s

Many Flemish weavers were encouraged to settle in England during Edward III's reign.

Social mobility increased in England as the rigid class structure of former times was gradually challenged; not least through the growth of a mercantile, middle class.

1315–17

The Great Famine in England (and across northern Europe) occurred after bad weather caused poor harvests, this was repeated in 1321. Consequent widespread unrest and criminal activity (including infanticide).

1316

A survey known as the *Nomina Villarum* recorded the names and lordship in every township under royal jurisdiction. (Published in six volumes).

1300
Population, 5 million

1306 (to 1329)
Robert the Bruce
of Scotland

1307 (to 1327)
Edward II

1314
The Scots, led by Robert the Bruce, routed the English at Bannockburn

1326
First Scottish Parliament

1327 (to 1377)
Edward III

1330s
Flemish cloth weavers encouraged to bring their skills to England

Socio-Cultural Timeline	Monarchy, State and Church

1336
Scottish raids caused considerable damage on Alderney and Sark

1337
The rank of Duke created

1337 (to 1453)
Hundred Years War against France began

1341

A valuation for taxation purposes was carried out called the *Nonarum Inquisitiones*. The results, which cover many counties, have been published.

1344 (or 1348)
Foundation of the Order of the Garter

1346
Battle of Crecy

1347
Calais captured and settled

1349
Ordinance of Labourers inaugurated English labour law

1347 (until 1350)

The Black Death (bubonic plague) caused a massive reduction in population numbers – as many as one third of men, women and children perished across England, Scotland and Wales.

1350
Population, 3 million

1350

As the plague subsided there was widespread movement of labourers and their families as workers sought (and could charge) more for their labour.

1351
The Statute of Labourers (Ordinance of Labourers) prevented workers moving in search of work, though thousands of serfs went to London in search of higher wages. The act ordered every town and village to erect a set of stocks for

1356
English victorious against the French at the Battle of Poitiers

Status of Children Born Abroad Act permitted children born abroad to two English parents to be English.

The earliest surviving churchwarden accounts date from the 1350s including Ripon and Hedon in Yorkshire, and St Michael's, Bath. (LRO)

c.1360

The oldest surviving road map of Great Britain called the Gough Map was produced – now in the Bodleian Library in Oxford.

1377

William Langland wrote his poem *Piers Plowman* that offers much information about medieval farming practices.

1377, 1379 and 1381

A Poll Tax levied on almost every individual in the land except paupers. In 1377 those eligible were aged 14 years and above, in 1379, 16 and above and in 1381, 15. Two thirds of the poll tax returns survive (TNA). They frequently give names and the relationships between taxpayers. Some lists included the names of heads of households as well as servants.

Socio-Cultural Timeline	Monarchy, State and Church
the punishment of unruly citizens	
	1360 Treaty of Brétigny marked the highpoint of English power in Europe. French recognised the English claim to Aquitaine and gave up all claims to the Channel Islands
1366 Statutes of Kilkenny forbad English settlers from adopting Irish law, custom, language or dress	
1369 Famine in England	
1370s Emergence of peasant farmers (yeomen class) with up to 100 acres	**1377 (to 1399) Richard II**

Socio-Cultural Timeline	Monarchy, State and Church	

1377 (until 1875)

Earliest records for the Court of Common Pleas (or Common Bench) survive, covering all actions between individuals that did not involve the king.

1381
Peasants Revolt, prompted by Poll Tax, occurred in towns and countryside

1382

Winchester College was founded; records of alumni survive and have been published in printed form.

1384
John Wycliffe, religious reformer and Bible translator, died

1385
The rank of Marquess created

1384 (to 1858)

Earliest wills proved by the Prerogative Court of Canterbury.

1386
The Wonderful Parliament

1387 (to 1400)
Geoffrey Chaucer wrote *The Canterbury Tales* in Middle English

1388 (until 1972)

Quarter Sessions began, dealing with legal issues at a local level, which meet four times a year. Records are usually found in county record offices though few survive from before the later 1500s.

The Statute of Cambridge restricted the movement of labourers and beggars and made the county divisions known as hundreds responsible for their own poor.

1399 (to 1461)
House of Lancaster

1399 (to 1413)
Henry IV
The Isle of Man under English rule

A survey of guilds and local fraternities was produced. The returns are held in TNA; those written in English have been published.

Chapter Five

1400s

1400s

By the early 1400s, most people in England would have used surnames that passed to their children. Hereditary surnames were just beginning to develop in Wales.

1400
Population, 3 million

c.1407
First mentally ill patients were admitted to Bethlem Hospital in London

1400 (to 1415)
Welsh revolt led by Owen Glendower

1405
The Isle of Man was granted to the Stanley family

1413 (to 1422)
Henry V

1415
Battle of Agincourt

1422

Records begin for Lincoln's Inn, the largest of the four Inns of Court.

1422 (to 1461)
Henry VI
(Plantagenet: House of Lancaster)

1429

The right to vote was given to all men over 21 years or those owning freehold land.

1434
River Thames froze

1437
Assassination of King James I of Scotland

1441

First documented African slaves brought into Europe.

c.1440
Johannes Gutenberg invented the printing press

1440
Rank of viscount created

Socio-Cultural Timeline	Monarchy, State and Church	

c.1450

A map of Goole Moor (Inclesmoor) and Thorne Moor in south Yorkshire was made in connection with a land dispute. (BL)

1450

| **1453**
Fall of Constantinople | **1453**
Loss of all French lands except Calais | Jack Cade's Rebellion, led against the policies of Henry VI, including the Statute of Labourers. |

1455 (to 1485)

War of the Roses

1461
Many thousands died during the Battle of Towton in Yorkshire

1461 (to 1470)
Edward IV
(Plantagenet: House of York)

1461-8
French ruled Jersey

1465

1470 (to 1471)
Henry VI (House of Lancaster restored)

Irish living near English settlements made to take English surnames

1471
Battles of Barnet and Tewkesbury

1471 (to 1483)
Edward IV (House of York restored)

Guernsey and Jersey were separated into two bailiwick administrations

1483–4

The College of Arms was founded to regulate heraldry and the granting of armorial bearings.

1483

Records made by heralds during their visitations (from 1530-1688) survive and many have been published.

1485

August–October: severe outbreak of sweating sickness in London killed thousands

1489

Parliamentary act to discourage land enclosure that was causing depopulation in some rural communities and was a major contributory factor in the abandonment of villages.

1495

Vagabonds and Beggars Act permitted punishment of the poor.

Licensing of alehouses began.

Socio-Cultural Timeline	Monarchy, State and Church
	1483 (April to June) **Edward V**
	1483 (to 1485) **Richard III**
	1485 Battle of Bosworth
	1485 (to 1509) **Henry VII** (House of Tudor)
1492 Christopher Columbus reached America	
Fall of Granada: Moors expelled from Spain	
1495 The first recorded instance in Europe of syphilis	
1497 John Cabot sailed from Bristol in search of a new route to the Orient	**1497** Cornish Rebellion
1498 Vasco da Gama landed on Natal coast (South Africa) then sailed to India	

Chapter Six

1500s

Socio-Cultural Timeline	Monarchy, State and Church
1506 Romani persons recorded in Scotland	**1509 (to 1547) Henry VIII** (House of Tudor)
	1513 Battle of Flodden Field
1515 Conversion of land from arable to pasture became an offence	
1517 Sweating sickness killed thousands, particularly students in Oxford and Cambridge	
Rise of Lutheranism	

1509

Government documents known as the *State Papers, Foreign and Domestic* have been published for the reign of Henry VIII and subsequent monarchs down to the late 18th century. They cover numerous social, as well as political, issues and name thousands of individuals. They have been published in calendar form.

1511 (to 1515)

A detailed manorial roll was produced for the Isle of Man (available in translation online).

1514 (to 1854)

Trinity House issued pensions to seamen and their families. Registers are extant from 1727.

1516

A parliamentary act designed to prevent the conversion in England and Wales of arable land to pasture.

1522

Muster Rolls began for local militias, listing adult males who were available for military service. The few that survive are held in TNA and LROs. A handful of county surveys have been published (Bucks, Cornwall, Gloucs., Rutland & Worcs.) as has the survey for the city of Exeter.

1523

The Great Subsidy was levied on all individuals over 16 years of age with land or goods worth £2 or an annual income of £1 or more. The returns contain very full lists of taxpayers. The original records are in TNA; some have been published.

1525

Admiralty records survive from 1525. (TNA)

1530

The Egyptians Act was passed to prevent gypsies from entering England and Wales. This introduced discrimination to those already here.

Socio-Cultural Timeline	Monarchy, State and Church
1519 Ferdinand Magellan began his circumnavigation of the world	
1525 Rebellions in the eastern counties due to the Amicable Grant	
1528 Sweating sickness killed thousands across England	

Socio-Cultural Timeline	Monarchy, State and Church

1530 (to 1688)

Heraldic visitations began to be undertaken across the country. Many have been published and provide a wealth of information for genealogists.

1530s (to c1700)

Inventories of personal estate often compiled for probate purposes. Many survive.

1534
Reformation of the English church began

1535
Beard tax purportedly imposed

1535

A thorough survey of church wealth, *Valor Ecclesiasticus* ('church valuation'), was made by royal officials in preparation for the Dissolution of the Monasteries. This applied to churches in England and Wales, plus parts of Ireland which were under English control.

1535 (and 1542)

Act of Union between England and Wales: The Welsh legal system was incorporated into the English system and English administrative practices were introduced by the Laws in Wales Acts.

1536

Divorce made possible in Scotland through the Commissary Court of Edinburgh.

1536
The Pilgrimage of Grace rebellion, prompted by opposition to the Dissolution of the

A poor law act passed allowing vagrants to be whipped.

1536 (to 1539)

The Dissolution of the Monasteries began whereby the small religious houses and later the larger ones, were systematically closed. Many monks and nuns found themselves homeless and the closure of religious houses exacerbated poverty as work opportunities and almsgiving dramatically decreased. Some 650 religious houses across England and Wales were closed.

Many of the redundant buildings (former monasteries, nunneries and so on) were sold, while others were given away by the King. Many minor noble families benefitted. The result was as much as one third of former church land across England and Wales was absorbed into royal and private hands.

1536 (to 1543)

Acts (of Union) were passed whereby English laws were imposed upon Wales. The Principality and Marches were joined to form a united Wales. Justices of the Peace were appointed for each of the seven counties and the English language was to be the only language used in the courts.

Socio-Cultural Timeline	Monarchy, State and Church
Monasteries, began in Lincolnshire and the East Riding of Yorkshire; 200 rebels were later executed	

Socio-Cultural Timeline	Monarchy, State and Church

1537

Foundation of Honourable Artillery Company, the oldest regiment in the British Army.

1538

The Exeter Conspiracy – an attempt to depose Henry VIII and replace him with a Yorkist; Henry Courtenay, 1st Marquess of Exeter

1538

Thomas Cromwell charged all clergy in England and Wales to keep records of all baptisms, marriages and funerals at which they officiated. Boyd's Index lists some 3.5 million English marriages from 1538-1837. Marriage Index provides names of bride and groom, the year and location of their marriage. (The original index can be searched online).

1539

John Leland began his journeys through England and Wales, which is published as *The Itinerary* in five volumes.

1540

Thomas Cromwell executed

1540

Statute of Wills permitted freehold land in England and Wales to be bequeathed. It also set a legal age for the writing of a will at 14 years for males and 12 for females (spinsters and widows only). This was eventually repealed and superseded by the Wills Act of 1837.

The Court of Wards now controlled wards (males under 21 and females under 14) and the administration of their lands. In 1542 it became the Court of Wards and Liveries. (TNA)

1542

The Crown of Ireland Act, passed by the Irish Parliament, declared that the new Kingdom of Ireland belonged to the monarchs of England. Parliaments of Ireland and England remained separate.

1542 (to 1830)

Court of Great Sessions established under the second Laws of Wales Act. The sessions met twice a year in each Welsh county to administer English law.

1547

The Vagabonds Act permitted the branding or enslavement of beggars who were deemed capable of work. Beggars incapable of working were to receive relief.

Many grammar schools for boys were founded during the reign of Edward VI.

Socio-Cultural Timeline	Monarchy, State and Church
1543 Nicolaus Copernicus published his *On the Revolution of Heavenly Spheres*	
1545 *Mary Rose* sank off Portsmouth claiming almost 400 lives	
1547 (to 1549) The Western Rebellion concerned protests in the southwest against the enforcement of Protestantism	**1547 (to 1553) Edward VI**

Socio-Cultural Timeline	Monarchy, State and Church
1549 Kett's Rebellion was a protest in Norfolk against enclosure that culminated in more than 3000 deaths	**1549** Book of Common Prayer introduced a new liturgy in church
1551 Last known serious outbreak of sweating sickness	
1552 Foundation of Christ's Hospital, Horsham, the first bluecoat school	
1553 (to 1554) Wyatt's Rebellion; a protest against the marriage of Queen Mary to Philip of Spain	**1553 (9 days)** **Lady Jane Grey** **1553 (to 1558)** **Mary**
1553 (to 1556) 280 Protestants were burned at the stake during Mary's reign	**1553** Catholic practices in church re-introduced

1549 (to 1550)

A tax on sheep was levied but was repealed within a year. Some records of ownership survive, though a proposed national census of sheep was never completed. The records can prove very useful when parish registers are unavailable.

1551

The Alehouse Act was introduced to combat increasing drunkenness. Licensees were required to enter bonds to ensure their customers orderly behaviour. The bonds were certified at Quarter Sessions and recorded. The act was repealed in 1828.

Gypsies required a licence in order to travel.

1552

A Poor Act passed which banned begging and authorised the appointment of a 'Collector of Alms' in each parish and created a register of licensed poor.

In Scotland all parishes were ordered to keep registers of baptisms and marriage banns. This was extended to include burials from 1565 and actual marriages from 1616. Adherence was patchy and few registers survive before the late 1600s.

1554

A second Egyptians Act designed to encourage Romani peoples to assimilate.

1555

Toll Books introduced at horse fairs recording buyers' names and where they came from.

1558

Recognised as the start date for parish records despite the fact that the instruction to keep registers had been given twenty years earlier. Parish records were now kept on parchment so the survival rate is greater than those previously recorded on paper.

1558 (to 1563)

The Statute of Artificers was a series of laws that were introduced to regulate labour issues. They included the setting of wages and placed limits on the free movement of workers.

Socio-Cultural Timeline	Monarchy, State and Church
	1554 (to 1558) **Philip** in the right of his wife Mary 1558 (to 1603) **Elizabeth I**
1555 Establishment of the Muscovy Company to trade with Russia	
A group of Africans were brought to London to learn English so that they could act as interpreters in Africa	
A Poor Act directed that licensed beggars should wear badges to indicate their status	
	1558 England lost possession of Calais
	1558 Protestant practices in church restored under Queen Elizabeth

Socio-Cultural Timeline		Monarchy, State and Church

1559

The Act of Uniformity laid the basis for the Protestant Church in England. Parishioners were required to attend church on Sundays. Thousands of Flemish (Walloon) and Dutch immigrants settled in London and the eastern counties during Elizabeth's reign, especially after the Dutch revolt of 1567, bringing with them their cloth-making skills.

Another Poor Law Act differentiated types of poor.

1560

In Scotland, Roman Catholicism was dis-established as the state church and replaced by the Church of Scotland, which would later be based on Presbyterianism.

In Scotland, probate jurisdiction was transferred from church courts to secular Commissary Courts under the Principal Commissariat of Edinburgh.

1562
The first of three slaving voyages undertaken by John Hawkins

1562

A law offers gypsies born in England and Wales the possibility of becoming English subjects provided they abandon their lifestyle and assimilate.

1563

An Act for the Relief of the Poor required parishioners to contribute to collections of alms or be turned over to the Justices of the Peace and fined.

1571

The holdings of each parish began to be regularly recorded. Surveys of land belonging to the church and inventories of ecclesiastical property, known as glebe terriers, were widely produced.

1572

The Vagabonds Act allowed Justices of the Peace to survey and register the impotent poor, establish how much was required for their relief and then assess parishioners who were required to pay rates.

Many Huguenots came to England in the wake of the Massacre of St Bartholomew's Day in France.

1573

Humphrey Llwyd's map of Wales, *Cambriae Typus*, published.

1574

A Scottish poor law act instituted some of the provisions made in English poor law such as making parishes responsible for provision of relief.

Socio-Cultural Timeline	Monarchy, State and Church
	1570s Growth of Presbyterianism
	1572 Thomas Howard, 4th Duke of Norfolk, tried for treason for his part in the Ridolfi plot to restore Catholicism in England

Socio-Cultural Timeline	Monarchy, State and Church	

1576
The first English theatre was built in Finsbury Fields, London

1576

The Bastardy Act gave powers to Justices of the Peace to issue Bastardy Orders and Bastardy Bonds whereby the father of an illegitimate child would be required to pay maintenance for its support.

Lambarde's *Perambulation of Kent* was published, the first county history with much of genealogical interest.

In Guernsey, a register of contracts was established including land transactions. Records are in French.

Another Poor Law act authorised counties to establish 'houses of correction' for vagrants and beggars, and set out the 'Punishment of the Mother and reputed Father of a Bastard'.

1579

Christopher Saxton completed a series of detailed and elaborate county maps for England and Wales. Saxton's maps were used by subsequent mapmakers.

1580
Congregationalists emerged as a Puritan sect called Brownists

1581
Dutch declared independence from Spain

1581

Recusancy (non-attendance at Anglican services, especially by Catholics) became a criminal offence punishable by heavy fines. Names of recusants appear in Quarter Sessions records and, from 1587-1606, in

Assize Court records. Defaulters were listed in the Recusants' Exannual Roll of 1581-1634/5.

1582

The Gregorian Calendar began to replace the Julian Calendar across Europe, adjusting dates by 10 days, shortening the year slightly and revising the pattern of leap years. Many countries had already standardized 1 January as New Year's Day. Reforms were not applied in England, Wales and Scotland until 1752. Adopted in parts of Ireland under English influence. Its use there died out by the 1640s.

1586

The first large-scale settlement of English people in Ireland occurred. This was called the Munster Plantation.

William Camden's *Britannica* published the first topographical survey of England.

1590

Chatham Chest Fund was established to pay pensions to Navy personnel. Records survive from the early 1650s. (TNA)

Socio-Cultural Timeline	Monarchy, State and Church
	1583 Newfoundland claimed as a colony of England
	1587 Execution of Mary Queen of Scots
	1588 A Spanish plan to invade England was scuppered when their naval fleet (armada) was destroyed
1590 (to 1591) North Berwick witch trials	

Socio-Cultural Timeline	Monarchy, State and Church	
	1591 Earl of Essex purchased the governorship of Alderney	**1592 (to 1691)** Annual Recusant Rolls of convicted Catholics compiled by the Exchequer. They are particularly extensive from 1663 to 1670 with over 10,000 entries, although these include many Protestant dissenters too.
	1595 Nine-Years War began in Ireland against England	
	The Raid of Mount's Bay (Battle of Cornwall) was a Spanish raid during the Anglo-Spanish War	
1597 Dublin gunpowder disaster Witchcraft hysteria in Scotland	**1597** Scottish king James VI (future King James I of England), wrote his views on witchcraft; *Daemonologie*	**1597** An Act for the Relief of the Poor required Churchwardens and Overseers of the Poor in each parish to levy a tax on parishioners in order to fund the provision of work for the poor; to assist those who couldn't work and to find apprenticeships for the young. Provisions under the Vagabonds Act meant male vagrants could now be drafted into naval service.

1598

Copies of all parish records were now to be sent annually to the local bishop. The copies are called Bishops' Transcripts and are useful when original parish registers have been lost or damaged.

Chapter Seven

1600s

Socio-Cultural Timeline	Monarchy, State and Church

1600s

Some records available from the early 17th century for the first indentured servants who went to the New World for work.

1600
English East India Company began to trade in the Far East

Population, 4.8 million

1600

Scotland adopted 1 January as New Year's Day instead of 25 March, as in England, Wales and most of Ireland. It continued to use the Julian Calendar.

1601 (to 1834)

The Poor Law placed a legal responsibility on each parish to care for those unable to work. The poor were classified into one of three groups by the Poor Law: the able-bodied poor, the impotent and persistent idlers. The able-bodied poor were offered work in houses of correction. Many records survive recording information on payments to the poor including rate books recording local rates paid by parishioners, Settlement Certificates, Bastardy Bonds, etc. The act also introduced parish apprenticeships for poor and orphaned children.

1601
Robert Devereux, Earl of Essex, executed for treason

Socio-Cultural Timeline	Monarchy, State and Church	
1602 (to 1795) Dutch East India Company founded	1603 (to 1625) James I (House of Stuart)	**1602** Richard Carew's *Survey of Cornwall*. Available online. The Land Registry was established in Jersey, with records in French.
	1603 Union of the Crowns of Scotland and England though the nations remain separate with their own Parliaments	**1603** Epidemic of bubonic plague in London.
	King James created many new peerages to encourage loyalty	**1604** A revised set of church laws, the Book of Canons, decreed that parental support was required for those under 21 years old to marry. In addition, the canons codified the system of granting licences to marry, necessitating an applicant to provide a bond and an allegation (or affidavit). Such bonds and allegations were filed and those that survive provide details about age, marital status and so on that is invaluable. The records after 1660 are particularly complete and are usually found in local archives. One third of the population of York died from plague.
	1605 Adoption of Union Flag for Great Britain	
	1605 Gunpowder plot after which Guy Fawkes executed	

1606

This year saw the beginnings of the Ulster Plantation as thousands of Protestants began to colonise north-east Ireland. At first this occurred privately but by 1609 the project had royal support and it is estimated that nearly 20,000 people settled. Concurrently many existing settlers moved within Ireland looking for land that better suited them.

1607

Jamestown established in Virginia, America; one of 13 colonies founded by the English before 1733.

1609

Bermuda colonised by the English.

1611

John Speed published *The Theatre of the Empire of Great Britaine,* which included the first set of individual county maps of England and Wales, plus maps of Ireland and a general map of Scotland. Speed's maps include hundreds, inset maps and some town plans.

Socio-Cultural Timeline	Monarchy, State and Church
1606 (until 1799) A Scottish act of Parliament bound miners in slavery to their masters	
1607 The Midland revolt followed by the Newton Rebellion	**1607** First Baptist congregation established in London
Some 2,000 people died during extensive flooding in the Bristol Channel	
1608 First recorded frost fair when the River Thames froze over.	
	1611 King James Bible published
	First Baronet created

Socio-Cultural Timeline	Monarchy, State and Church

1612

Trial of the Pendle Witches in Lancashire.

1615
Arbella Stuart, England's 'lost queen', starved herself to death in The Tower of London

1616
Death of William Shakespeare

1615

Penal transportation of miscreants to colonies in North America and the West Indies was more regularly used. Alphabetical lists of convicts who were transported between 1614 and 1775 have been published.

1617 (to 1858)

Register of Sasines recorded land conveyance in Scotland. It was the first public register of deeds and can be searched online through Registers of Scotland.

1618
The Company of Adventurers of London Trading with ports in Africa

1618
Sir Walter Raleigh executed

1618

A hundred destitute children were transported from London to augment the colonial population of Virginia.

1618-48
Thirty Years War led to massive death toll in German lands

1620

One hundred Puritan separatists, later dubbed the 'Pilgrim Fathers', sailed for America on the *Mayflower* where they established Plymouth Colony.

1621
Publication of the first English news sheet, the *Corante*

1621
James I gave Canada to Sir Alexander Sterling

1622
First record of bottled spring water at Holy Well Spring, Malvern

1622
The island of St Kitts became the first English settlement in the Caribbean

1622 (to 1641)

The first English newspaper called the *Weekly News* began. Foreign news only.

↑

**1625 (to 1649)
Charles I**

1625
Barbary pirates
raided Mount's Bay,
Cornwall and took
60 men, women and
children into slavery.

1626
Further attacks on
Cornish ports by
Barbary pirates.

Acidic waters at
Scarborough led to
an interest in the
benefits of 'taking
the waters' and the
development of
other spa towns

1627

The colonisation of Barbados
began. The majority of emigrants
to the Americas over the following
decades lived on the island, many as
indentured servants.

1628

The island of Nevis in the West Indies
was colonised.

1628 (to 1862)

Records of Fleet Prison, Marshalsea
Prison, King's Bench Prison and
Queen's Prison began. (TNA)

1630

The Muster Rolls of Ulster, recorded
the principal landlords in the province,
with the names of Protestant men
whom they could call up if needed.
The rolls are in the BL but lists of
names can be found online.

1630
Population 5.6
million

1630s
Public
stagecoaches
began to provide
links with London
within a 30-mile
radius of the city

↓

Socio-Cultural Timeline	Monarchy, State and Church

700 Puritans left Southampton for America, eventually settling in Massachusetts. Some 20,000 more emigrated to New England in the 1630s, the peak of the 'Great Migration'. By 1700 the population had reached 92,000.

1634

The Irish House of Commons passed an Act for the Punishment of the Vice of Buggery

1634

In Ireland, all Protestant baptism, marriage and burials began to be recorded in Church of Ireland registers. Where parishes complied, often marriages were also included. Many Catholic and other Protestant churches unofficially performed these rites for their members, but few such records survive from before the early 19th century.

The Stent Records of Inverkeithing are amongst the earliest Scottish land valuation documents to survive.

The colony of Maryland was established in America to provide a refuge for Catholics, although many settlers would be Protestant.

1634 (to 1640)

Charles I's Ship Money Tax was levied without parliamentary support and with mixed results. It was a tax on property designed to raise funds for maritime defence and was traditionally levied on coastal towns. This unpopular tax was levied countrywide.

Many tax schedules have survived (in BL and LRO) and name individuals. A few schedules have been published.

1641

Irish Rebellion

1641 (to 1642)

As a result of the many plots against King Charles I and unrest in Parliament, a Protestation Oath was introduced. The act required all adult males in England and Wales to declare allegiance to the King, Parliament and the Protestant religion. The names of those who refused to sign were noted. About one third of returns survive in the House of Lords and have been published. Counties are listed alphabetically and then by parish and hundred; some counties are better represented than others.

1642

The Collection for Distressed Protestants in Ireland listed many women and recorded oaths of loyalty made to the King. The returns, of which about one third survive (also in the House of Lords), are organized by parish.

Civil war interrupted keeping of parish registers.

Socio-Cultural Timeline	Monarchy, State and Church
	1639 (to 1653) Wars of the Three Kingdoms began with the Bishops' Wars in Scotland
	1640 'Long Parliament' began
1641 Newspapers, which included news from home, began to proliferate as censorship ended	
1642 Unrest in Ulster; 50,000 killed	**1642 (to 1651)** English Civil War began
1642 (until 1660) All theatres were closed to prevent public disorder	Oxford the Royalist base until 1646 The pitched Battle of Edgehill in October between Royalists and Parliamentarians was inconclusive

Socio-Cultural Timeline	Monarchy, State and Church	

1642 (to 1660)

The Committee for Advance of Money and Compounding Tax was established to investigate the wealth of individuals for the purposes of forcing loans. After August 1646 only Royalists were forced to pay.

1643
Licensing Order passed by Parliament to censor newspapers

1643 (to 1664)

The Committee for Plundered Ministers was established to investigate the political loyalties of church ministers and increasingly acted against those men who supported Charles I. The Sequestration Committee was also set up to confiscate the property of Royalists who continued to fight for the king. The Committee for Compounding with Delinquents dealt with issues concerning the recovery of sequestrated property belonging to Royalists who agreed not to take up arms against Parliament. (TNA)

1644
July. Royalists defeated by Parliamentarian troops at the Battle of Marston Moor

1644

First register of the Congregational Church.

1645
Barbary pirates captured 240 men, women and children from Cornwall

Great Plague in Edinburgh killed up to half the city's population

1645
The Battle of Naseby followed by the Battle of Langport. The last Royalist field army was

decimated. West Country fell to the Parliamentarians

1646

Westminster Confession of Faith

1646

The abolition of The Court of Wards and Liveries brought wardship and other ancient practices to an end.

1647

London Corporation established to build workhouses and houses of correction for the indolent poor, to enforce laws against vagabonds and to set the poor to work. (www.workhouses.org.uk)

Earliest Baptist registers survive from this date

1648

Quakerism began, founded by George Fox; registers of members were regularly kept by the 1670s.

1648 (to 1649)
Second Civil War

1649

Siege of Drogheda – massacre of Catholic citizens by Oliver Cromwell's troops.

1649
Execution of Charles I

Establishment of the Commonwealth. Many Royalists fled abroad

1650

Repeal of the Act of Uniformity led to the rise of many non-conformist groups.

1650s
Ireland's population decreased from 1.3 to 1 million owing to the effects of the Cromwellian wars

Socio-Cultural Timeline	Monarchy, State and Church	
Frequent pirate attacks along the South West coast threatened England's fishing industry		Formation of Coldstream Guards, oldest continuously serving regiment in the British Army.
1651 The first coffee house in England opened in Oxford	**1651** **Charles II** crowned at Scone but went into exile in France	**1651** The Battle of Worcester brought an end to the Civil War. Some 8,000 Scottish soldiers captured at Worcester were deported to the Americas to work as indentured labourers. Approximately 3.7 per cent of the English population and 6 per cent of the Scottish died as a result of the Civil War.
1652 Dutch East India Company established Cape Colony at Table Bay	**1652** First Anglo-Dutch War, mostly fought at sea	**1652** Cromwell's (Catholic) opponents were stripped of land in Ireland under the Act of Settlement of Ireland. The lands were re-distributed.
1653 The Great Fire of Marlborough in Wiltshire destroys houses and the town's textile industry	**1653 (to 1660)** The Protectorate **1653 (to 1658)** Oliver Cromwell became Lord Protector of the Commonwealth of England, Scotland and Ireland Barebones Parliament	**1653** During the Commonwealth, civil registers of births, marriages and deaths officially replaced parish registers of baptism, marriages and burials in England and Wales although some parish registers continued to be kept. Few civil registers survive from this period Provincial probate courts abolished with probate now granted in London only.

1653 (to 1660)

Civil marriage introduced by the Marriage Act.

Period dubbed by genealogists the Commonwealth Gap owing to the paucity of records that were kept or that have survived from this period.

1654

A register survives (in print and online) of names of 10,000 indentured servants who left from the port of Bristol for the New World between 1654 and 1686. Servants were drawn from across Britain. (Available online)

1655-6

The Down (or Civil) Survey was carried out which mapped Ireland. The original maps were lost to fire but copies survive in various collections and have been published in print and online.

1656

The Edict of Expulsion rescinded, officially permitting a small community of Sephardic Jews to settle in England, although a small community had been established in 1541.

Socio-Cultural Timeline	Monarchy, State and Church
	1654 (to 1660) Anglo-Spanish War caused by commercial rivalry
	1655 British captured Jamaica from the Spanish
1656 *Musaeum Tradescantianum,* the first museum open to the public established in Lambeth	

Socio-Cultural Timeline	Monarchy, State and Church	

1657

Earliest surviving Roman Catholic registers but few were kept before 1700 and most date from after the late 18th century. In Ireland, Catholic registers were not widely kept until the 1830s.

1658
Hurricane storms in southern England; the worst for centuries

1658 (to 1659)
Richard Cromwell now Lord Protector

1659

Pender's Census in Ireland recorded the names of owners and details of land holdings. Surviving records have been published.

Start of monthly national meteorological Mean Central England Temperature data collection; available online.

1660
The Royal Society founded to promote the discussion of matters of scientific interest

First entry in Samuel Pepys' diary

1660 (to 1707)
Charles II (House of Stuart restored)

1660 (to 1685)
Charles II

1660
Many new peerages were created by Charles II including dignities granted to his mistresses and their families

The Tenures Abolition Act brought an official end to feudalism

1660

A poll tax was levied on all men and women over 16 years of age annually until 1697.

Commonwealth registers end, parish registers resume and provincial probate courts were re-established.

Records for Naval Officers began after administrative reorganisation by Samuel Pepys.

A few British began to settle in the Dutch controlled Cape Colony in South Africa.

The first regular standing army established.

1660 (to 1902)

Naval passing certificates awarded to officers on their successful completion of examinations, were inaugurated.

1661

A (voluntary) tax entitled 'A Free and Voluntary Present to Charles II' was levied, for which returns for more than 30 counties survive.

1661 (to 1828)

The Corporation Act prevented non-Anglicans from holding municipal office by requiring oaths of allegiance to the Crown and Church of England and the annual taking of Anglican communion.

1662

The Quaker Act made it illegal to refuse to take the Oath of Allegiance.

An Act of Uniformity passed this year led to the establishment of many places of education for nonconformists including Bristol Baptist College.

The Settlement Laws came into force permitting newcomers to an area to be evicted if a complaint was made against them within 40 days of arrival. The law reduced the mobility of the poorer classes and discouraged those without work to search for employment elsewhere. If a man

Socio-Cultural Timeline	Monarchy, State and Church
	1660 The English Navy becomes the Royal Navy
	1661 Bodies of Oliver Cromwell and Henry Ireton exhumed and posthumously executed
1662 Bury St Edmunds witch trials	**1662** Charles II sold Dunkirk to France

Clarendon Code (including the Act of Uniformity) required all English and Welsh clergy to accept the Book of Common Prayer |

Socio-Cultural Timeline	Monarchy, State and Church

left his own parish, he had to take a Settlement Certificate with him which guaranteed that his home parish would cover any return costs that he might incur if he began to claim poor relief.

The Settlement Act also required gypsies to be baptised.

Limits to rights to claim poor relief.

1662

The Book of Common Prayer outlined the prohibited marriage list. Marriage between cousins was still permitted.

1662 (to 1689)

A Hearth Tax was imposed by Parliament to support Charles II and his household. A shilling was to be paid twice yearly for every hearth (or stove) in all domestic dwellings. Subsequent amendments permitted exemptions. From 1663 all hearths, whether taxable or not, were listed. The tax returns reveal the size of dwelling in which the payee lived. (TNA E179)

1663
The first turnpike road was authorised for a section of the Great North Road

1664 (to 1667)
Second Anglo-Dutch War began after the Dutch surrendered Fort Amsterdam in New Netherland to the English

1664

The Conventicle Act forbade religious meetings of more than five people in an effort to discourage non-conformity.

	Socio-Cultural Timeline	Monarchy, State and Church

1664 (to 1815)

Impressment to the navy was now officially authorised.

1664
Formation of the Admiral's Regiment (known as the Marines from 1802)

1665

Oxford Gazette (later *The London Gazette:* www.thegazette.co.uk) founded; carrying much of interest to the genealogist, including a record of appointments to public office, issues of insolvency and appointments and resignations of military officers, awards of gallantry medals, etc.

A non-conformist burial ground, called Bunhill Fields, opened in London (Records in TNA).

1665
Great plague of London killed more than 60,000 – the last serious visitation of plague in England

1665
Five-Mile Act – restrictions on nonconformist ministers

1666 (to 1814)

The Burial in Wool Act meant that woollen shrouds were now to be used, with a £5 fine for non-compliance, though paupers were exempt. Parish registers were often annotated to show payment or exemption. The directive tended to be ignored from the 1770s.

1666
Great Fire of London

1667 (to 1853)

The earliest Ships' Muster Books began recording financial issues and act as a form of service record. (TNA)

1667
Publication of John Milton's *Paradise Lost*

1667
A significant defeat of the Royal Navy with the Dutch raid on the River Medway

1668 (to 1920)

Naval Officers' Pay Books. (TNA)

Socio-Cultural Timeline	Monarchy, State and Church	

1669

First Lutheran registers kept. (LMA)

1670

Hudson's Bay Company founded leading to the establishment of trading posts in Canada

Population 5.7 million

1670

Divorce by act of parliament was introduced in England and Wales, but just 318 successful cases were heard by 1858 and only four cases were brought by women. Annulments and separation decrees were available through church courts, but decrees did not permit re-marriage.

1671

A Board of Customs established

Earliest Synagogue registers.

1672

The Royal African Company was founded to regulate the English slave trade

1672

High Court of Justiciary established in Scotland

1672 (to 1674)

Third Anglo-Dutch War – army increased to 10,000 men

1672

Charles II's Royal Declaration of Indulgence in March loosened some of the strict laws against nonconformists. Certain penal laws were suspended and the building of some non-conformist chapels was permitted.

In Scotland, workhouses were to be established for the employment of able-bodied beggars. Charity workhouses were later founded for the relief of those individuals who could not work.

1673

The Test Act came into force, enhancing the regulations imposed by the Corporation Act of 1661 and ensuring that nonconformists could not hold public office. The Act was frequently renewed leading to various 'Returns of Papists' over the following century.

An act was passed permitting the calling of Special Constables on a temporary basis in response to a rise in public disorder.

1673 (to 1849)

Naval Succession books introduced to ships – listing warrant and commissioned officers. (TNA)

1674

Records for the Old Bailey began and are useful for the detail they provide of defendants, their lawyers and witnesses. Proceedings up to 1913 are available online. (www. oldbaileyonline.org)

1675

John Ogilby's *Britannia Illustrata* includes 100 strip maps of the chief roads in England and Wales.

1676

The Compton Census, named after Henry Compton, Bishop of London, attempted to find the numbers of Anglican conformists, Roman Catholic recusants and Protestant dissenters in England and Wales.

1674
Treaty of Westminster ends the Third Anglo-Dutch War

1675
To curb political activity Charles II issued the 'Proclamation for the suppression of Coffee Houses'

1676
Charles II and Louis XIV signed the secret Treaty of Dover. The English king agreed to convert to Catholicism and assist the French

Socio-Cultural Timeline	Monarchy, State and Church

in their attempt to conquer the Dutch Republic
in their attempt to conquer the Dutch Republic

Information was collated by ecclesiastical parish. The returns have been published and some (including those for Norwich) are available online.

1676 (to 1772)

The Ordinary of Newgate's Accounts began. They are detailed records made by the chaplain (or Ordinary) of Newgate prison and relate, for example, final conversations with criminals. They are available online.

1677

Samuel Lee's list of merchants living in and around London was published as *The Little London Directory*. It names almost 2000 merchants and goldsmiths involved in the wholesale trade and is available online.

1678 (to 1681)
The conspiracy to assassinate Charles II, fabricated by Titus Oates, led to the execution of 15 men and widespread anti-Catholic hysteria

John Ogilby and William Morgan published their *Large Scale Map of the City as Rebuilt By 1676*. Engraved across 20 sheets, this was the first accurate map of London showing buildings in plan and not as bird's eye views. (Copy in BL and available online).

1680
The Great Comet was the first to be identified by a telescope

c.1680

Headstones began to be regularly used to mark the place of burial in churchyards.

1682

The first English settlers arrived in the province of Pennsylvania after its establishment the previous year by Quaker, William Penn.

Travels of Celia Fiennes (to 1712) whose diaries have been published and provide detailed information on English towns and properties she visited.

1684

The Royal Hospital Kilmainham in Dublin was founded to house retiring soldiers and to administer the pensions of those leaving service in Ireland.

1685

The Edict of Nantes was revoked by the French king, Louis XIV which resulted in the renewed persecution and killing of many Huguenots; thousands fled to England to escape persecution.

Registers of Huguenots began.

The Bloody Assizes, a series of trials that began in Winchester and moved to Salisbury, Dorchester, Taunton and Wells were held. More than 1,400 individuals who had been involved in the Monmouth Rebellion between May and July were tried. Hundreds of rebels were executed, and many were transported to the West Indies.

Socio-Cultural Timeline	Monarchy, State and Church
1683-4 The Great Frost. A frost fair was staged on the River Thames	**1683** The Rye House Plot against Charles II
	1685 (to 1688) James II
	1688 The Glorious Revolution
	1688 William III (to 1702) and **Mary II** (to 1694)
	1689 (to 1692) Jacobite uprising in Scotland in support of the exiled James II
	1690 Battle of the Boyne
	1692 Massacre at Glencoe

Socio-Cultural Timeline	Monarchy, State and Church

1686

Newton wrote *Mathematical Principles of Natural Philosophy*

1689 (to 1697)

Legislation passed to encourage the consumption of gin rather than French brandy.

1689 (until 1815)

With the surrender of the privilege of neutrality, Guernsey privateering began

1687

The Settlement Act of 1662 was amended as it now became necessary to establish settlement by occupying a property valued at more than £10 per annum, for more than forty days.

1689

The Toleration Act permitted nonconformists to worship, provided they licensed their meeting places.

1690

Berrow's Worcester Journal founded, the oldest continuing local newspaper in the world.

1691 (to 1856)

Naval Ratings' Pay books begin. (TNA)

1692

Scottish clansmen sympathetic to the Jacobite cause were killed in the Glencoe Massacre

1692

The Royal Hospital, Chelsea, London, was founded to house retiring soldiers and to administer the pensions of those leaving military service in Britain. (TNA)

1693 (to 1963)

A new land tax was introduced after a county valuation was carried out, to assess who and what was taxable. A few early returns survive, though most postdate 1780. (TNA and/or LRO)

	Socio-Cultural Timeline	Monarchy, State and Church
	1694 The Bank of England was founded by Royal Charter.	**1694** Queen Mary died from smallpox
	1694 (to 1699) Poll Tax imposed in Scotland	
	1694 A storm wrecked several ships in the Strait of Gibraltar, including HMS *Sussex*: more than a thousand drowned	
	1695 Martin Martin; *A Description of the Western Islands of Scotland*	**1695** Parliament did not renew the statutes requiring press censorship
	1695 (until 1699) Large-scale emigration from Scotland following famine, especially to Ireland	

1695

First Dissenter lists in parish registers recording the names of children born but not christened in the Anglican church.

1695 (until 1869)

Greenwich Hospital, London was founded as a home for retired naval seamen.

1695-6

Marriage Duty Act levied a tax on births, marriages and deaths and charged a poll tax on unmarried bachelors! Evidence suggests a rise in Fleet marriages for expedience and cost. Led to the 1753 Marriage Act (Hardwicke's) to close loopholes. Surviving records name householders and dependants.

Socio-Cultural Timeline	Monarchy, State and Church

1696

The French king, Louis XIV lent ships and men to the exiled James II to help him regain his kingdom. When the plot failed a lengthy series of trials followed generating widespread interest

The government attempts to deal with clipped, hammered and damaged coinage by passing the Recoinage Act

A Board of Trade established to manage British financial affairs in the colonies

1696

Following a plot to assassinate William III, Association Oaths were introduced requiring all those in public office (civil, religious and military and all adults in some British colonies) to swear loyalty to the Crown. Many others, including some women, appear voluntarily on the Oath Rolls. Some records are available online.

County Sheriffs were now required to compile poll books recording the names of those who had voted in elections. The lists also indicate which candidate the voter supported. The elector's address and property entitling his vote is sometimes recorded. The survival rate for poll books improved after 1711.

Bristol Corporation of the Poor formed by local Act for the purpose of the setting up of workhouses. Other places later followed this example; Exeter in 1697 and Colchester in 1698.

1696 (to 1851)

A Window Tax replaced the Hearth Tax leading to widespread bricking up of windows. Occupiers of dwellings were required to pay the tax rather than owners. A few records for England and Wales survive though many survive for Scotland.

1697

A Marriage Act directed that all interfaith marriages would be considered as Catholic.

A further Settlement Act extended and developed the system of granting certificates and made it possible for the migrants to resist removal whilst looking for work.

The Act made it mandatory for paupers to wear badges indicating their status. The badge comprised a capital P plus the first letter of the name of their parish. Failure to display the badge could result in punishment.

1698 (to 1703)

A tax imposed on entries in parish registers. Rescinded after five years.

Socio-Cultural Timeline	Monarchy, State and Church
1697 An act authorised the erection of inscribed waymarkers on roads	
1698 SPCK established to foster better manners and encourage establishment of charity schools The Royal African Company monopoly ended, allowing private traders from Bristol and Liverpool to operate Fire destroyed Whitehall Palace in London	**1698** Treaty of the Hague signed between France, England and Holland
1699 The first slave ship sailed from Liverpool	**1699** Parliament limits the country's standing army to 7,000 'native born' men

Chapter Eight

1700s

Socio-Cultural Timeline	Monarchy, State and Church
1701 Population 6 million	**1702 (to 1707)** **Anne**
	1702 Many new peerages were created by Queen Anne
1703 The Great Storm caused severe damage across southern England and killed 10,000	
1705 Thomas Newcomen patented the steam engine	**1704** Battle of Blenheim
	1706 Suzerainty of the Isle of Man passed to the Duke of Atholl
1707 The Scilly naval disaster saw four warships lost in bad weather	**1707** Act of Union established the Kingdom of Great Britain

1702

Manuscript army lists began – for officers. (TNA)

First daily newspaper, *The Daily Courant*, published by Elizabeth Mallet in Fleet Street every day until 1735 when it was merged with *The Daily Gazetteer*.

1704

The Penal Code barred Catholics from voting, education and the military.

A Deeds Registry was established at Wakefield, in the West Riding of Yorkshire. It contains over a million records of property ownership. The registry was followed by the East Riding in 1708, Ireland in 1708, Middlesex in 1709 and the North Riding of Yorkshire in 1735.

1708

Earliest Artillery Muster Rolls. (TNA)

1709

In March the Act for the Naturalisation of Foreign Protestants was passed, by which immigrants could pay a small fee in order to become naturalised. It was directed specifically at French Huguenots who had come to England and whom the government was keen to support.

Between May and November, some 13,000 'Poor Palatine' immigrants from German speaking lands arrived in England. Many were unskilled agricultural labourers and their arrival caused disquiet. Some were encouraged to travel on to North America.

1710

The first policy registers made in connection with fire insurance in London began. They gave the names of policyholders, details of the properties insured and any tenants. Registers can be found in local record offices and the Guildhall in London has a good collection.

1710 (to 1804)

A Stamp Act introduced a tax on Apprentice Indentures, except where

Socio-Cultural Timeline	Monarchy, State and Church
1708 (to 1709) The coldest winter in centuries	**1708** Abortive invasion of Scotland by the Old Pretender supported by the French
1709 Poor harvests and famine across Europe; bread riots in Britain. A period known as Great Frost or The Great Winter. *The Tatler* founded The first recorded inter-county cricket match played between Kent and Surrey	**1709** Anglican clergyman Henry Sacheverell achieved nationwide fame after preaching a sermon at St Paul's that was distributed in print and led to riots and his trial
	1710 The British take permanent possession of Nova Scotia

Socio-Cultural Timeline	Monarchy, State and Church

the fee was less than 12d and with a few other exceptions. The indentures often name the father of the apprentice together with his address and occupation.

1711

1712
Last trial for witchcraft in England held in Hertfordshire.

Thomas Newcomen's steam driven piston engine provided efficient pumping of mines

1713
Treaty of Utrecht by which Spanish ceded Gibraltar and French ceded Newfoundland to Britain. Under the treaty, Britain was awarded the *Asiento*, the sole right to import an unlimited number of enslaved people to the Spanish Caribbean for 30 years

John Ecton published his *Liber Valorem et Decimarum*, a directory of ecclesiastical benefices which lists patrons and incumbents.

An Act required that poll books be deposited with the Clerk of the Peace. Many poll books for elections survive from this date until the last election for which they were made in 1868.

1714
Jethro Tull perfected the seed drill

1714 (to 1901)
House of Hanover

1714 (to 1727)
George I

1714

The Hanoverian accession led many Germans to settle in England and an increase in Anglo-German relations.

1715
World's first wet dock in Liverpool with capacity for 100 ships

1715 (to 1716)
First Jacobite rebellion mostly in Scotland

1715

Register of Papist Estates, established to facilitate additional taxation or forfeiture. Most entries survive up to 1725. The register was in force until 1778 and not fully abolished until 1791. Also from 1716, wills of Catholics were registered in the Close Rolls.

In Ireland, county militias were established with membership restricted to Protestants.

1718

The Transportation Act introduced the official removal of convicts to lands overseas. Between 1718 and 1776, more than 50,000 convicts were transported to North America. Transportation to America ended when war began between Britain and American colonists.

The Edinburgh Courant newspaper, with national coverage, was now published regularly. Followed by *The Caledonian Mercury* in 1720.

1718 (until 1728)

Bishop Kennett encouraged the keeping of detailed entries in parish registers by incumbents in his diocese of Peterborough.

1723

Knatchbull's Act (The Workhouse Test Act) enabled workhouses to be erected by parishes.

Universal oath of loyalty imposed. Rolls with names of loyal subjects were drawn up. (LROs)

Socio-Cultural Timeline	Monarchy, State and Church
1717 The Masonic Grand Lodge of London and Westminster established	
1718 The first factory in England opened in Derby producing silk	**1718** The Religious Worship Act restored some freedoms to Dissenters
1720 Widespread speculative investment in previous years collapsed with the South Sea Bubble ruining hundreds	**1719** An abortive Jacobite invasion, supported by the Spanish
	1721 (to 1742) Britain's First Prime Minister, Sir Robert Walpole, Whig
	1723 The Black Act added 50 capital offences to the penal code, including some forms of poaching

Socio-Cultural Timeline	Monarchy, State and Church

1724 (to 1726)

Daniel Defoe's compilation of observations, *A Tour through the whole island of Great Britain*, published.

1725
The Grand Lodge of Ireland was established

1727 (to 1760)
George II

1728
Vitus Jonassen Bering reached Alaska

1729
The first of five parliamentary acts designed to curb the consumption of gin, was passed

1730
Severe famine in Ireland

1730s
Growth of first seaside towns including Brighton and Margate

Charles 'Turnip' Townsend promoted Norfolk four crop rotation which would revolutionise agricultural productivity

1731 (to 1868)

Publication began of *The Gentleman's Magazine*, an invaluable source for contemporary society, which includes biographical details of individuals.

1731
The first Circulating Schools in Carmarthenshire encouraged literacy

1732

Earliest cavalry and infantry Muster Rolls. (TNA)

Unmarried mothers expected to name the father of their illegitimate child under oath during a Bastardy Examination.

	Socio-Cultural Timeline	Monarchy, State and Church
1733 The use of Latin in public records was abandoned in favour of the English language.	**1733** Invention of the flying shuttle which revolutionised weaving	**1733** The Sugar and Molasses Act was passed to tax British colonists in North America
1734 Brown and Kent's *Directory of the Cities of London and Westminster and the Borough of Southwark* published. It is available online.	**1734** Approximately 6,000 Jewish people living in England	
1735 In Sutherland, Scotland, Lieutenant Hugh MacKay was ordered to procure Highlanders to settle in Georgia. (The orders to Mackay are online with names of some transportees).	**1735 (to 1749)** The Hawkhurst smugglers active across the south east of England **1736** The Grand Lodge of Scotland was established	
	1738 Highwayman Dick Turpin hanged	**1738** The Fetter Lane Society, a precursor to Methodism, founded
1739 Formation of Methodist Societies in and around London; though official break with Anglicanism came in 1784. *The Scot's Magazine*, originally called the *Edinburgh Magazine*, was founded which includes birth, marriage and death notices and is still published.	**1739-40** The Great Frost in Britain	**1739** George Whitefield and John Wesley began preaching at outdoor rallies **1739 (to 1748)** War of Jenkin's Ear

Socio-Cultural Timeline	Monarchy, State and Church

1739

Hundreds of Scottish Clan members were rounded up and sold as indentured servants to landowners in the Carolinas in North America.

1740

Thousands of clandestine marriages were taking place annually in the vicinity of Fleet prison in London

1740

Protestant Householder returns made in Ireland. Transcripts of the original records survive for the counties of Antrim, Armagh, Down, Donegal, Londonderry and Tyrone and list the names of heads of households and are arranged by barony and parish. (PRONI and NAI)

1740-41

Severe famine in Ireland led to thousands of deaths and fuelled food riots

1741 (until 1954)

The Foundling Hospital opened in London, with outposts elsewhere, housing some 27,000 children.

Earliest Moravian register for Fetter Lane congregation in London.

1742 (to 1743)
Earl of Wilmington, Spencer Compton, Whig

1743 (to 1754)
Henry Pelham, Whig

1742 (to 1837)

The Baptists, Presbyterians and Independents form a General Register of births of Protestant Dissenters of the Three Denominations. In 1768 baptisms were added. The central registry for births for the three denominations is called Dr William's Library.

1744

An illegitimate child, who previously took the parish of birth as its place of settlement, now took the same place of settlement as its mother. This prevented mothers and children being separated if they became paupers.

1746

John Rocque's very large and detailed map of London was published. (Copies are held in various libraries and it can be accessed in print form and online).

1747 (to 1782)

A tax was imposed on all horse-drawn carriages, legislation which was extended in the early 1770s to cover steam-powered vehicles.

1749

Census of Elphin records details of households across Roscommon and parts of Galway and Sligo.

1751

Army introduced regimental numbers instead of being named after the colonel in charge and were soon after given official titles such as the 'King's Own'.

Socio-Cultural Timeline

1744
HMS Victory sank off the coast of Guernsey with the loss of more than 1,000 men

1750
Two earthquakes in London in the spring caused panic

Population
6.5 million

Monarchy, State and Church

1745
Jacobite Rebellion began as Charles Edward Stuart (Bonnie Prince Charlie) attempted to regain the British throne for his father, the Old Pretender

1746
The Jacobites were defeated at the Battle of Culloden

Socio-Cultural Timeline	Monarchy, State and Church	
	1752 Parliament passed a bill to bestow estates forfeited by Jacobites to the Crown	**1752** 14 September – England and Wales adopt the Gregorian calendar, thus moving from Wednesday 2 September to Thursday 14 September. The start of the year moves from 25 March to 1 January (New Style). Beware when interpreting dates! Forced clearances of tenants in the Scottish Highlands began. Some 20,000 emigrate over the next decade and many move into the burgeoning cities such as Glasgow.
1753 The British Museum founded Bow Street Runners appointed to patrol London's streets		**1753** Jewish Naturalisation Act permitted Jewish people to become naturalised as British citizens but was repealed after one year due to widespread opposition. Legal restrictions on Jews ended in the mid-nineteenth century. The Licensing Act inaugurated the recording of full registers of victuallers – to be kept by the Clerk of the Peace at Quarter Sessions.
	1754 (to 1756) Duke of Newcastle, Thomas Pelham-Holles, Whig	**1754** Hardwicke's Marriage Act introduced to counter irregular or clandestine aka 'Fleet' marriages. Now, a marriage was supposed to take place in the parish in which either the bride or groom had been born. Each party was to be 21 years of age or to have parental

consent. All couples (except Jews and Quakers) had to marry in a licensed (Anglican) church. Ready printed books for: name of bride and groom, their parishes, current marital status, date of ceremony, names of witnesses and officiating minister. Banns or marriage licence recorded either with marriage record or separately. Irregular Marriages continued until 1949 in Scotland at, for example, Gretna Green.

1754 (to 1879)

First printed annual Army Lists produced.

1756 (to 1777)

A tax introduced on silver plate for which some returns survive. (LRO)

1757 (to 1831)

The Militia Act revived county militias in England and Wales. Extensive military records survive from this date. Annual lists were made in each parish of all adult males between the ages of 18 and 50. Names, occupation, infirmities and, after 1802; number of children listed. By this act 30,000 men were raised between 1757 and 1763. (Some records at LRO)

Socio-Cultural Timeline	Monarchy, State and Church
1755 Lisbon earthquake caused tsunami in Cornwall three metres high	
1756 Britons died in the Black Hole of Calcutta	**1756 (to 1757)** Duke of Devonshire, William Cavendish, Whig
Privateering started from Alderney	**1756** Seven Years War against France began
	1757 (to 1762) Duke of Newcastle, Thomas Pelham-Holles, Whig

Socio-Cultural Timeline	Monarchy, State and Church
	1758 England began to govern in India, laying the foundations of the Empire
	1759 General Wolfe captured Quebec from the French
1760 The Industrial revolution underway	**1760 (to 1820)** King George III
1760s On his farm near Loughborough, Robert Bakewell began pioneering innovative agricultural practices including selective breeding of sheep	
1761 (to 1830) The Bridgewater Canal was the first to open followed by a period of 'canal mania'	
John Harrison's chronometer was perfected, allowing determination of longitude at sea	
	1762 (to 1763) Earl of Bute, John Stuart, Tory

1760

Army Regimental Records began though few survive before c.1794. (TNA)

1761

Parliamentary Land Enclosure Acts (c.1750 to c1845) increased as landowners sought to legalise enclosure of their property. The character of the landscape and its accessibility by the ordinary person were transformed.

1761 (to 1994)

The army began to keep registers of births/baptisms and marriages (Chaplain's Returns). (GRO)

1762

A parliamentary act required that records were kept within metropolitan parishes of parish poor infants.

First Unitarian registers.

1763

Mortimer's Universal Directory (for London) included the names of retail shops.

Sketchley's Directory of Birmingham published.

1763 (until 1790)

Yorkshire clergyman, William Dade, kept unusually detailed parish registers and his practice was adopted elsewhere.

1765

Benjamin Donn produced a detailed map of Devon (one inch to the mile), with maps of other west country counties in following years.

1766

Religious census of Ireland. Church of Ireland clergy were ordered by the Irish House of Lords to compile complete returns of all heads of households in their parishes.

1763 (to 1765)
George Grenville, Whig

1764
James Hargreaves perfected a technology he called the Spinning Jenny

Lloyd's Register of Shipping

House numbering introduced to London

1765
Isle of Man Purchase Act gave rights over the island to the British

1765 (to 1766)
Marquess of Rockingham, Charles Watson-Wentworth, Whig

1766 (to 1767)
Earl of Chatham, William Pitt the Elder, Whig

1767 (to 1770)
Duke of Grafton, Augustus Fitzroy, Whig

Socio-Cultural Timeline	Monarchy, State and Church	
		Hanway's Act required that all pauper children under 6 from metropolitan parishes be sent to school in the countryside. This meant children were separated from parents.
		The number of windows that incurred tax was raised to seven.
		1767
1768 Foundation of The Royal Academy which admitted a mix of classes to its exhibitions		A Return of Papists (a list of Catholics) compiled at the instigation of parts of the press to engender anti-Catholic feeling.
1769 Captain James Cook claimed New Zealand for Britain Richard Arkwright patented his water frame		
1770s A rise in grain prices saw the potato began to usurp bread as a staple of the working-man's diet	**1770 (to 1782)** Lord North, Frederick North, Tory	**1770** Records of prisoners kept from 1770 to 1894. (TNA and available online)
1770 Captain Cook landed in Botany Bay		
1771 First water powered mill heralds the beginning of mass-production in factories		

	Socio-Cultural Timeline	↑	Monarchy, State and Church

1772

The British Nationality Act allowed citizenship to be assumed if the father was British.

First Navy Lists published.

First *Morning Post* published on a daily basis until 1937. The *Morning Post* was well known for its coverage of society and cultural events.

Elizabeth Raffald's *Directory of Manchester and Salford* published, listing traders, manufacturers and some inhabitants with appendices listing officials, carriers etc.

1772
The movement to abolish slavery gathered momentum after the emancipation of a slave in England resulting from the Somerset v Stewart case in the English Court of King's Bench

The black population of London numbered approximately 10,000

1773

Edinburgh's earliest directory published.

1773
Captain Cook reached Antarctica

1774

Madhouse Act, which remained in force until the Mental Health Act of 1959, required all madhouses to be licenced. The act was designed to counter abuses including the imprisonment of those who were not insane but had been rejected by their spouse.

1775
Watt's steam engine patented

1775
American War of Independence

1776

Arthur Young's *Tour in Ireland* published. Early copies included much social detail.

1776
Declaration of Independence by America

1776
A parliamentary act allowed decommissioned ships to be used as prison hulks

Socio-Cultural Timeline	Monarchy, State and Church

1777
Reformer John Howard publishes *The State of the Prisons in England and Wales* based on his observations

1777 (until c.1812)

William Markham, Archbishop of York, encouraged Dade's scheme (*see* 1763) to be practised throughout his diocese. Dade registers are invaluable for genealogists.

1777 (to 1852)

A tax imposed on male servants. Schedules are to be found in TNA and NRS.

1777 (1778 and 1791-2)

Lists made of those living on Gibraltar.

1778
James Cook and George Vancouver were the first Europeans to land in British Columbia

1778
Louis XVI of France declared war on Britain

1778

Catholic Relief Act. Lifting of anti-Catholic laws in England, Wales and Ireland. In Scotland, The Protestant Association prevented similar legislation. (*See also* 1791)

1779

The Penitentiary Act authorised state prisons in preference to transportation or the death penalty.

c.1780
Robert Raikes opened the first Sunday school in Gloucester for poor children offering basic literacy and religious instruction

1780

Pallot's Marriage Index records 1.5 million marriages celebrated in many parishes until 1837 covering most London parishes and some further afield. (Available online)

	Socio-Cultural Timeline	↑	Monarchy, State and Church

Pallot's Baptism Index records some 200,000 baptisms in Greater London up to c.1837. (Available online)

Methodist registers began. (JRL)

c.1780 (to c1842)

Bankruptcy case files available at TNA.

Further schools began to open

1780
The Gordon Riots erupt in London in protest against the Catholic Relief Act, hundreds died.

Construction began of Manchester's first cotton mill

1781
More than 130 Africans were thrown into the sea near Jamaica by British slavers in the Zong Massacre

1782

Start of name index to Sun Insurance Fire Policy records at LMA (to 1842).

Gilbert's Act allowed parishes to form unions to maintain workhouses to house the elderly and infirm.

First issue of Steele's Navy List gave names of serving officers. Superseded by Navy Lists in 1814.

1782
The Central Atlantic hurricane hit a British fleet with considerable loss of life

1782 (to 1783)
Earl of Shelburne, William Fitzmaurice, Whig

1782 (to 1782)
Marquess of Rockingham, Charles Watson-Wentworth, Whig

1783 (to 1794)

Stamp Duty Act introduced a tax on baptisms, marriage and burials. It did not apply to paupers, and parish registers were often annotated to

1783
Volcano Laki in Iceland erupted with catastrophic consequences for European weather, leading to many deaths in late summer

1783 (to 1784)
Duke of Portland, William Bentinck, Whig

Socio-Cultural Timeline	Monarchy, State and Church	
		show payment or exemption. The introduction of the tax resulted in a fall in the number of entries overall, but an increase in the number of those described as paupers.
		The Treaty of Paris created the United States. About 75,000 people loyal to Britain leave America, mostly settling in Canada.
		Glasgow's earliest directory published.
1784 The threshing machine was invented First mail coaches introduced	**1784 (to 1801)** William Pitt the Younger, Tory	**1784 (to 1807)** A Game Tax was levied on all qualified to kill or to sell game. Taxes imposed on the owners of horses used for transport and racehorses. Both repealed in 1874. The Window Tax levied in England and Wales was introduced to Scotland where to this day blocked up windows are called 'Pitt's Pictures' after the prime minister who oversaw its introduction. Quarry Bank Mill in Styal opened, where half the workforce were young apprentices who produced cotton cloth. **1785** First edition of *The Times*.

1785 (to 1792)

A tax on female servants for which some schedules survive in TNA and NRS.

1787

Eleven ships sailed from Portsmouth in May carrying more than 700 prisoners and some free settlers to Australia.

1788

The First Fleet arrived in Botany Bay in January 1788 and established the first penal colony in Australia.

Hasted's *History of Kent* (to 1799).

1791

Catholic Relief Act. Further relaxation of anti-Catholic laws which applied to England, Wales and Scotland. Similar legislation took effect in Ireland in 1793.

Socio-Cultural Timeline	Monarchy, State and Church
1788 The Dolben Act regulated the slave trade	
1789 The French Revolution began – French émigrés arrived in Britain	
1790 John McAdam invented a new surfacing treatment for roads	
The first decennial census was held in the United States, though only the head of the household was named.	
1791 Thomas Paine's *Rights of Man* published	**1791** The Canada Act divided the country into Upper and Lower Canada

Socio-Cultural Timeline	Monarchy, State and Church	
		The *Universal British Directory* published in five large volumes. The directory was a forerunner to the VCH and included geographical and historical details on counties as well as notes on schools and other facilities plus lists of inhabitants with trades. Subsequent copies list street directories and names of householders.
1792 Ross-shire riots in July (Year of the Sheep) when tenants protested against Highland Clearances	**1792** First Regency Crisis	**1792 (to 1799)** Richard Horwood published his very detailed map entitled *Plan of the Cities of London and Westminster*, which aimed to show every property. The 32 sections of map measure more than 4m across when placed together. (Copies at BL and available online). A wave of emigration to North America from Scotland occurred as thousands were forcibly evicted from the land.
1793 The Aliens Act was passed to regulate the numbers of refugees fleeing France for Britain	**1793 (to 1802)** Britain at war against France	**1793** In response to the French wars, the Aliens Act was introduced (another in 1798) which established a system of registering aliens at ports of entry. Registration was abolished in 1852 and the Act was repealed in 1905. Irish militia reorganized; officer ranks were restricted to Protestants, but Catholics now permitted to join the other ranks.

The Friendly Societies Act laid down the rules under which societies could operate.

1794

A Tour of Cambridgeshire, the first of Charles Vancouver's reports for the Board of Agriculture was published. Further reports on Essex (1795), Devon (1808) and Hampshire (1813) were published and contain invaluable detail for the counties and farming practices.

The government under William Pitt instigated trials in England of leading political radicals. More than thirty men were arrested and many emigrated.

1795

The Speenhamland system of poor relief was introduced (until 1834) in some parts of the southern counties offering financial assistance linked to the price of bread.

Quota Acts were introduced which forced counties to supplement recruitment to the navy. Numbers provided varied from one part of the country to another – London had to provide an additional 5,700 men – but tens of thousands of men were required. Many petty criminals were used to make up the numbers. Indexed returns are kept in TNA and give the names and physical descriptions of men.

1794
Treason trials

1795
Food riots and widespread famine in England after a poor harvest and high prices owing to war

British invasion of the Cape Colony, South Africa. (Returned to the Dutch in 1803)

Socio-Cultural Timeline	Monarchy, State and Church	
		1795 (to 1869) A tax of one guinea a year was levied on hair powder. Taxpayers received a certificate from the local Justice of the Peace. Some certificates can be found in LROs and give full names and position in a household.
1796 First vaccination by Edward Jenner against smallpox The Retreat opened near York pioneering a more humane approach to the treatment of people with mental health problems	**1796** Work began on Norman Cross Prison near Peterborough in Huntingdonshire, the first purpose-built prisoner of war camp	**1796** Chaplain's Returns began recording baptisms, marriages and burials at stations overseas (to 1880). Available online. The Spinning Wheel Premium Entitlement List, or Flax Growers Bounty List, is an index of names of individuals across Ireland and in particular Ulster. It was drawn up in connection with a government initiative to encourage the linen trade by granting spinning wheels to those who planted flax on their land. The list is available online. The Supplementary Militia Act raised an additional 64,000 men, by ballot (in effect the first period of conscription), from across the country to serve in the war against France. **1796 (to 1882)** A tax on the keeping of dogs; expressly limited to persons keeping sporting dogs or a number of dogs. (LRO)

1796 (to 1906)

Death Duties were introduced as a tax which was now liable on the estates left by a deceased person. Initially property transferred by legacy was taxed by way of a Legacy Duty. As the tax threshold was lowered in subsequent years more people were liable to pay. Indexed death duty registers (in TNA, with some early examples online) are often filled with detail that is of interest to the family historian.

1796 (to 1994)

The Army began recording deaths of serving personnel. (See Army Chaplains' Death Indexes, TNA and GRO)

1797

Scottish militia was re-established by Act of Parliament.

1797
Battle of Fishguard (French invasion by 1400 troops)

1798

Income Tax introduced with further taxes between 1803-16 and 1842 to present! :(

With imminent threat of French invasion, the authorities in Buckinghamshire drew up the *Posse Comitatus* giving details of all able-bodied men and assets. The returns have been published.

1798
Thomas Malthus published *An Essay on the Principle of Population*

1798
Uprising in Ireland – English militia volunteered for service in Ireland

Socio-Cultural Timeline	Monarchy, State and Church

1798 (to 1880)

A tax on armorial bearings. All the nobility, old and new, were required to register their coats of arms, and pay for a licence to seal their letters with their arms.

1799
Slave Trade Act restricted involvement in the slave trade to the ports of London, Bristol and Liverpool

1799

15,000 Irish militia joined the regular army in Britain.

1799 (to 1824)

The Combination Act banned early trade unions.

Chapter Nine

1800s

	Socio-Cultural Timeline	Monarchy, State and Church

1800

The Census (or Population) Act made it possible for the first census of England, Wales and Scotland to take place.

		1800 Acts of Union were passed in 1800, though the United Kingdom incorporating Ireland wasn't formed until 1 January 1801

1801

Tuesday 10 March – National Census. Prompted in part by the panic caused by Malthus's predictions published in his *Essay on the Principles of Population*. Information was gathered parish by parish but no detail was collected on individual households. Local officials provided information on the number of inhabited and uninhabited houses in a parish, numbers of people who lived, their types of employment and numbers of baptisms, marriages and burials.

The first one-inch to one-mile map (of Kent) was published by the Ordnance Survey.

	1801 Population, 16.3 million	**1801** Inclosure (Consolidation) Act
		1801 (to 1804) Henry Addington, Tory PM

1801 (until 1849)

Prison ship (hulks) registers available. (TNA)

	1802 Health and Morals of Apprentices Act introduced to improve conditions for apprentices working in cotton mills	**1802** One-year lull in hostilities between Britain and France during which travel to the Continent resumed

Socio-Cultural Timeline	Monarchy, State and Church
1803 In the US, President Thomas Jefferson made the Louisiana Purchase	**1803** Lord Ellenborough's Act made abortion a crime
1804 First railway steam locomotive	British begin settling Van Diemen's Land
Napoleon became Emperor of France	**1803 (to 1815)** War between Britain and France resumes; continual fear of invasion
1804 (to 1812) Martello towers were built to defend England from possible French invasion	Napoleonic Wars – 1/6th of all British men served in the army or navy
	1804 (to 1806) William Pitt the Younger, Tory PM
	1805 Battle of Trafalgar

1803

Debrett's Peerage first published.

The Passenger Vessels Act was passed in order to regulate the transport of immigrants and emigrants and to ensure some level of safety. The act encouraged better sanitary arrangements on board ship and improvements in the provision of food and comfort. However, costs of emigration rose, making it difficult for ordinary people to emigrate until the act was repealed in 1826.

1803

Naval pensions now paid via Greenwich Hospital.

1803 (to 1804)

Parish constables drew up a list of men aged between 17 and 55 who might be called upon as a reserve force. Between 1803 and 1813, almost 100,000 militiamen joined the regular army.

1805

The Battle of Trafalgar. A database exists online naming all the servicemen who participated in the battle which is available via TNA.

1806

A purpose built Military Academy opened in Woolwich for the training of officers.

1808

County Asylums Act was passed, designed to encourage the construction of private asylums for the mentally ill. The first asylum opened in Northampton in 1811.

1810

John Lockie's *Topography of London* was published which offered concise descriptions of every square, street, lane, court and much more in London.

1811

Monday 27 May. A national census was held, following the format used ten years earlier. Enumerators were now asked to explain why houses were uninhabited so that the prosperity of a given district could be judged more accurately.

Socio-Cultural Timeline	Monarchy, State and Church
	1806 Napoleon attempted an economic blockade of Britain
	1806 (to 1809) Lord William Grenville, Tory PM
	1806 Cape Colony ceded to the British
1807 The import and use of slaves in Britain was outlawed but slavery continued in the colonies	**1807 (to 1809)** Duke of Portland, William Bentinck, Whig PM
	1808 (to 1814) British Army involved in the Peninsular Campaign in Spain
1809 The Preventative Water Guard established	**1809 (to 1812)** Spencer Perceval, Tory PM
1810 Badging of the poor was officially repealed	
1811 Population, 18.5 million

The Christmas Gale wrecked several Royal Navy ships and some 2,000 men were drowned | **1811** The Prince of Wales became Regent |

Socio-Cultural Timeline	Monarchy, State and Church

The National Society for Promoting Religious Education was founded with schools opening across the country providing basic tuition based on the teachings of the Church of England for the very poor. The schools, which were usually located near the parish church, were later absorbed into the state system.

1811 (to 1812)
First occurrence of Luddite activity in Nottingham

1811 (to 1820)

Further Highland Clearances.

1812
Gas lamps were now widely used for lighting streets

1812
Framebreaking Act imposed the death penalty for Luddites

1812 (to 1827)
Earl of Liverpool, Robert Jenkinson, Tory PM

War of 1812 began, fought between the UK and US, ending in 1815

1812

In England and Wales, Rose's Act introduced ready-made printed forms for baptism and burial records. Baptismal records contain: name of child, mother's name (not maiden name – see 1903 and 1911), father's name; occupation and residence, date of baptism, name of clergyman. Burial records were now more detailed recording the name of the deceased, age, residence, date of burial and the name of the officiant. The act came into force on 1 January 1813.

Some 250 regiments of local militia existed with more than 200,000 men enrolled.

Slave registers were introduced on plantations in the British Caribbean. The registers were discontinued after the abolition of slavery.

1813
The United Grand Lodge of England was formed

1814

James Pigot began publishing national directories, which are useful for the information they provide on professional people, nobles, gentry and clergy, coach and carrier services (http://specialcollections.le.ac.uk/digital/).

Navy Lists began recording officers' names; published quarterly.

1815

The Battle of Waterloo, which saw the final defeat of Napoleon, was the first campaign where the soldiers who had participated were issued with special medals. The names of soldiers are recorded in medal rolls (Available online). The practice of impressment to the Royal Navy officially ended.

1816

Large-scale emigration to North America from Ireland as 6,000 left, followed by a similar number the following year.

1817

Johnstone's London Commercial Guide and Street Directory printed.

Socio-Cultural Timeline	Monarchy, State and Church
1814 (and 1816) Further outbreaks of Luddism	**1814 (until 1822)** Robert Peel established the Peace Preservation force in Ireland and, soon after, a system of county constabularies
1815 As war with France ended, demobilisation of the army led to mass unemployment Napoleon exiled First of the Corn Laws passed, helping farmers but with disastrous impact on the poor	**1815** A decisive defeat of Britain by the US at the Battle of New Orleans
1816 Dire harvests due to poor weather, caused widespread hunger in this 'Year without a Summer'	
1816 (to 1826) 10,000 British troops based in India died during the first cholera pandemic	**1817** National outpouring of grief after the death of the Princess of Wales in childbirth

Socio-Cultural Timeline	Monarchy, State and Church

1817 (until 1830)

The Greenwood brothers published a series of large-scale folding maps of most English counties. Exceptions were: Bucks, Cambs, Herefordshire, Herts, Norfolk, Oxon and Rutland.

1818 (to 1994)

The army began to record marriages of serving personnel.

1818

The first well-documented ragged school, designed to benefit the poor, opened in Portsmouth.

1819

Singapore became a new trading post

1819

Peterloo Massacre left 15 dead and several hundred injured. The Relief Fund Account Book lists the names of 350 individuals who received assistance payments. (JRL)

1820s

Temperance societies began in Scotland and Ulster, soon spreading to other parts of the UK

1820 (to 1830)

George IV

1820

Publication of county directories began which continued until the early 20th century.

First Europeans, including British, began to settle in New Zealand.

1821

Monday 28 May. A national census was held following the format used in 1801 and 1811. Enumerators were now required to enquire about age in order that the government might establish how many men would be available to bear arms if necessary. The question was also designed to help improve the tables on which life assurance was based.

First census held in Ireland. Most census records for the period 1821-1891 were later destroyed. Some fragments survive – for parts of Armagh, Cavan, Fermanagh, Galway, Meath and Offaly (then known as King's County).

1822

Between 15 September 1822 and 26 March 1823, some evidence of age was necessary when application was made for a licence to marry. Usually a baptismal certificate was supplied for this purpose. The change was, however, short-lived and was abandoned.

1823

The residential requirement for marriage whereby either the bride or groom had to have been resident in a parish for four weeks was reduced to fifteen days.

Socio-Cultural Timeline	Monarchy, State and Church
1821 Population, 20.9 million Michael Faraday invented the electric motor	
1821-32 Greek War of Independence attracted British including Lord Byron to the cause	
1822 Work began on the Cardiff Docks from whence coal and iron was exported	**1822** George IV's celebrated visit to Edinburgh promoted national identity, including the adoption of tartan by clans HM Coastguard founded
1823 Proclamation by the US president of principles that became the Monroe Doctrine	

Socio-Cultural Timeline	Monarchy, State and Church

The age of consent returned to pre-1753 levels with 14 for boys and 12 years for girls. Consequently fewer underage couples went to Scotland to marry and generally married in their own parish.

The first Mechanics' Institute opened in London – and in Ipswich and Manchester the following year – offering educational opportunities to adult workers. Hundreds more would open across the country.

Tithe Applotment books began in Ireland listing landholders including tenant farmers and lessees.

1824
Society for the Prevention of Cruelty to Animals established

1824

The Combination Acts were repealed enabling workers to establish trade unions.

Quarterly prison returns, from 1824 to 1876, record the offence, date, place of conviction and term of sentence.

In Scotland, the probate of testaments was transferred to county Sheriff Courts.

1824 (until 1879)

Hulks and Prisons Quarterly Returns. (TNA)

1825
Stockton and Darlington Railway opened – the first public steam railway in the world

1826

White's first commercial directory published for Hull; listing trades peoples' names and addresses.

Burke's Landed Gentry (originally called Burke's Commoners) and *Burke's Peerage, Baronetage and Knightage* were published by John Burke after years of genealogical research by members of his family. Revised editions have been published down the years until 1972.

1827

Greenwood's Map of London published.

1828

Test and Corporation Act was repealed, allowing Catholics and Dissenters to hold public office.

1828 (to 1861)

Perry's Bankrupt and Insolvent Gazette published monthly.

Socio-Cultural Timeline	Monarchy, State and Church
	1825 Authority over Alderney passed to the Crown
1827 Publication of *The Shepherd's Calendar* by John Clare, a poetic account of the contemporary farming year Burke and Hare's first murders in Edinburgh	**1827 (to 1827)** George Canning, Tory **1827 (to 1827)** Viscount Goderich, Frederick Robinson, Tory
1828 An Act to Regulate the Carrying of Passengers in Merchant Vessels passed to regulate safety for emigrants to the colonies	**1828 (to 1830)** Duke of Wellington, Arthur Wellesley, Tory

Socio-Cultural Timeline	Monarchy, State and Church

1829
The first 'bobbies' appointed by Sir Robert Peel

Stephenson's steam locomotive, *Rocket*, won the Rainhill Trials

1830
The Liverpool and Manchester Railway opened

Revolution in France and riots across Europe

The Swing Riots in southern England

Bus mania in London as horse-drawn omnibuses proliferated

Beer Act led to free trade in the brewing industry

1830 (to 1834)
Earl Grey, Charles Grey, Whig

1830 (to 1837)
William IV

1829

In Ireland, all Catholic baptisms, marriages and deaths were to be recorded at parish level though this was not always the case.

The Catholic Emancipation Act removed penalties against Catholics and led to the building of many Catholic churches and the return of monasticism in England.

1830s

A steep rise in the numbers of people who left Britain for good, in particular those who had been affected by agricultural depression. Many sailed from the port at Liverpool.

1830

Mormonism has its origins in the Church of Christ founded by Joseph Smith on 6 April in New York. Mormon belief in baptism for the dead has given rise to their interest in and support of genealogy.

The Plymouth Brethren, whose origins can be traced to Dublin around 1827, were established at a meeting in Plymouth. In 1849 they split into Open Brethren and the Exclusive Brethren.

William Cobbett's detailed account of the English countryside was published as *Rural Rides*.

Responsibility for divorce cases in
Scotland transferred to the Court of
Sessions.

1831

Sunday 29 May – National Census.
Enumerators were now required to ask
about occupations. Only Londonderry
returns survive for Ireland.

The Parish Register Abstract was
compiled which collated details about
all parish registers pre-dating 1813. It
was printed and is available online.

1831 (to 1848-9)

Publication of Samuel Lewis's
Topographical Dictionary of England,
providing detail on towns and villages
across the country and arranged
alphabetically by place.

1832

Electoral registers were compiled for
the first time, naming qualified voters,
residence, and ownership of property
in a polling district.

Parliamentary Act to encourage
establishment of private cemeteries
was passed.

The Great Reform Act was passed
which brought significant change
to the electoral system as 'rotten
boroughs' were abolished. The number

Socio-Cultural Timeline	Monarchy, State and Church

1831
The Royal
Geographical
Society was formed
in London 1831

The first occurrence
of cholera in Britain
(Sunderland)

Population,
24.1 million

1831 (to 1832)
Collapse of the
November Uprising
led to the first major
influx of Polish
people

1832
Approximately
55,000 people died
of cholera

1832 (to 1833)
Beginnings of the
Oxford Movement

Socio-Cultural Timeline	Monarchy, State and Church

of those eligible to vote increased to about one million men, although qualification remained largely based on property values. Electoral registers were introduced, listing qualified voters, residence and the basis of voting entitlement. The registers were compiled annually except between 1916-17 and 1940-44.

1833

A Factory Act attempted to regulate working hours in the textile industry

Charles Babbage designed the Difference Machine – a forerunner of the modern computer

1833

The abolition of slavery occurred in the British Colonies. England freed 780,993 slaves.

Canada, as part of the British Empire, became a destination for American slaves escaping on the 'Underground Railroad'.

1833 (also 1846)

Samuel Lewis's *Topographical Dictionary of Wales* followed the format of the dictionary of England and included detailed maps.

1834
The Tolpuddle Martyrs

1834 (to 1834)
Viscount Melbourne, William Lamb, Whig

1834 (to 1834)
Duke of Wellington, Arthur Wellesley, Tory

1834 (to 1835)
Sir Robert Peel, Tory

1834

The Poor Law Amendment Act saw English and Welsh parishes grouped together as Poor Law Unions and the construction of more than 300 workhouses over the next five years. Outdoor relief forced all paupers into workhouses. There was considerable opposition to the system particularly in northern England. (Records are in LRO)

1834
Houses of
Parliament in
London burnt
down, witnessed by
thousands

1835

The Marriage Act forbade marriages
between closely related individuals, in
particular a man and his dead wife's
sister (*see* 1907). Some couples married
abroad to evade the law.

The Municipal Corporations Act
(or Municipal Reform Act) reformed
local government in 178 incorporated
boroughs in England and Wales.
Unincorporated towns, such as
Birmingham, could now request
incorporation. The councils in such
towns were now to be elected by men
who had paid rates for at least three
years. The names of these ratepayers
(or burgesses) were recorded in rate
books. (TNA and LRO).

The Merchant Shipping Act meant
that all crew lists were to be logged.

1836

The Tithe Commutation Act
abolished the ancient system of
paying tithes in goods. Fixed charges
were introduced, ending in 1936.
Tithe maps, of which some 12,000
survive, give the names of owners and
occupiers of land and were prepared
across the country in 1840.

1835
The first
photographic
negatives exposed
by Fox-Talbot

Christmas became
a national holiday

London City Mission
founded

1835
Mount St Bernard
established; first
Catholic monastery
built in England
since the middle
ages.

1835 (to 1841)
Viscount Melbourne,
William Lamb, Whig

1836
Great Trek began
as Dutch settlers left
the British controlled
Cape in South Africa

1836
Irish Constabulary
Act provides central
organisation for the
police in Ireland

Socio-Cultural Timeline	Monarchy, State and Church	
		The General Register Office for England and Wales established with a Registrar General.
		Establishment of London University as a secular alternative to Oxford and Cambridge Universities. Records of alumni have been published.
1837 Euston opened as the first London railway station	**1837 (to 1901)** **Victoria**	**1837** 1 July – Civil registration of Birth, Marriages and Deaths (BMD) began in England and Wales. A single governmental register instead of church records based on administrative poor law unions. However, registration of births was not made compulsory until 1874. It was now possible for a marriage to be performed in a certified building other than a church.

1837

1 July – Civil registration of Birth, Marriages and Deaths (BMD) began in England and Wales. A single governmental register instead of church records based on administrative poor law unions. However, registration of births was not made compulsory until 1874. It was now possible for a marriage to be performed in a certified building other than a church.

Samuel Lewis's *Topographical Dictionary of Ireland* was published, providing a highly detailed description of towns and villages in Ireland and is an important account of the country before the Great Famine.

The Wills Act raised the legal age for writing a will to 21 years. Nuncupative wills (made by word of mouth on a deathbed) were now only valid for members of the armed forces who died in action.

By the Slave Compensation Act, hundreds of former slave owners were given payments by the British

Government. (Lists of former slave owners are online www.ucl.ac.uk/lbs/search/).

1837 (and 1838)

Burke's Commoners of Great Britain and Ireland published, containing details about individuals who owned land or held high official rank but were not considered nobility.

1838 (until 1939)

Publication began of *The Era*, a weekly newspaper which came to specialise in the report of sport, freemasonry and theatre.

1838 (until 2003)

The Public Record Office was established in Chancery Lane as the repository for public records in the United Kingdom.

Irish Poor Law Act established a system of workhouses and a Poor Rate levy to pay for them.

1839

The Custody of Infants Act allowed mothers to petition the courts for custody of their young children up to the age of seven years and to have access to older children.

Socio-Cultural Timeline	Monarchy, State and Church
1838 Chartist petitions began (the first, signed by 1.2 million people was presented to Parliament in 1839)	
Outbreaks of smallpox killed tens of thousands (until 1841)	
Samuel Morse demonstrated the telegraph	
1839 (to 1844) Rural protests called the Rebecca Riots in Wales	**1839** County Police Act allowed voluntary establishment of rural forces (see also 1856)
1839 A commercial photographic process called the daguerreotype is introduced	Opium Wars with China began

Socio-Cultural Timeline	Monarchy, State and Church
1840 Height of railway mania	**1840** New Zealand was brought into the British Empire
Introduction of the Penny Black stamp	
The United Province of Canada was established	

1840

The Outdoor Relief Prohibitory Order restricted assistance given to the poor outside the workhouse.

Civil registration of births, marriages and deaths began on the islands of Guernsey, Herm and Jethou though record keeping was in practice patchy in the early years.

Henry Mayhew described the condition of the London poor in a series of articles for the *Morning Chronicle* (published in 1851).

Socio-Cultural Timeline	Monarchy, State and Church
1841 The first excursion by rail organised by Thomas Cook	**1841 (until 1907)** New Zealand became a Crown colony
Richard Beard opened England's first photographic studio in Regent Street, London	**1841 (to 1846)** Sir Robert Peel, Tory
Population, 26.8 million	

1841

Sunday, 6 June, National Census. First national census to record more detailed information and is the earliest census generally used by family historians. Full name, sex, and age of those under 16 years of age was given exactly, but those over 16 were rounded down to the nearest unit of 5. Enumerators also recorded the occupation of people living in a household. Many seasonal workers were not included. Only the returns for Cavan survive for Ireland.

Publication began in London of *The Jewish Chronicle*, a weekly newspaper rich in genealogical information.

The Morpeth Testimonial Roll, signed by 160,000 Irish, as a gesture of appreciation to the departing Chief Secretary of Ireland. It is a useful census substitute.

1842

Civil registration began in Jersey.

First edition of *The Illustrated London News*, the first illustrated weekly newspaper. It included all kinds of topical news (British and foreign) including stories about crime and social issues. The newspaper also carried details of births, marriages and deaths and advertisements. It was published weekly until 1971 and then less frequently until its closure in 2003. An archive is available online.

Mines Act outlawed employment of women, and children under 10, in mines.

Military pensions were now paid through local offices instead of the Royal Hospitals.

1844

The Naturalisation Act – procedure for naturalisation was simplified.

The Companies Act required registration of all companies.

Factories Act restricted hours of work for women and children. Registers were now to be kept listing child employees.

Friedrich Engels published *The Condition of the Working Class in England* based on his observations in Manchester.

Socio-Cultural Timeline

1844
Railways Act extended rail travel. 200,000 navvies were employed to construct lines across the country, all the main lines were complete by 1852

Monarchy, State and Church

1842
Britain gained Hong Kong

Thousands of British servicemen and civilians died during the retreat from Kabul during the First Anglo-Afghan War

1843
New Zealand Wars

1844
Bank Charter Act allowed only the Bank of England to issue banknotes

Socio-Cultural Timeline	Monarchy, State and Church
1845	**1845**
The Great Hunger (famine) in Ireland. Over 1 million people died and thousands of Irish migrants moved to Liverpool with approximately 25 per cent of the city's population Irish born by 1851. Two million Irish emigrated to the US over the next 10 years	General Inclosure Act
Collapse of a bridge in Great Yarmouth killed 80	
The ironworks such as Dowlais in Wales were at their height, employing thousands including many Englishmen who migrated for work	
The Andover Workhouse Scandal	

1845

Kelly's Directories began which supplement the information given in other directories with lists of some individuals, arranged by address, social status and profession. (http://specialcollections.le.ac.uk/digital/)

The Lunacy and County Asylum Acts were passed describing those with mental illness as patients. Officials called Masters in Chancery were given the task of establishing and inspecting asylums. Many mentally ill individuals incarcerated in workhouses were removed to asylums.

Ireland lost 16% of its population between 1845 and the end of famine in 1852.

The first Medical Directory was published with names, addresses, qualifications and other details on general practitioners.

A Scottish Poor Law Act established Parochial Boards under the direction of the central Board of Supervision to collect and distribute funds to those in need of support and unable to work. Poor houses could be set up at the discretion of the Boards in large parishes or groups of parishes.

Civil registration of non-Catholic marriages began in Ireland.

After 1845, cause of death was generally certified by a doctor.

1846

Samuel Lewis's *Topographical Dictionaries* of Scotland published.

1847

The Consolidated General Order was instituted, regulating life in workhouses across the country.

1847 (to 1865)

Griffith's Valuation Lists recorded every land and householder in Ireland, with a description of their property. (NAI and also printed).

1847 (to 1886)

Assisted emigration to Australia began. Some (but not all) passenger lists survive and some have been made available online.

1849

Civil registration of births and marriages began on the Isle of Man but was voluntary.

First edition of the quarterly *Notes and Queries* was published containing much of genealogical interest. An archive is available online.

The first edition of *Who's Who* was published; a compilation of biographies of prominent Britons. It

Socio-Cultural Timeline	Monarchy, State and Church
1846 Very hot summer gave rise to many epidemics	**1846 (to 1852)** Lord John Russell, Whig
1847 A typhus epidemic killed more than 30,000	
1848 Year of Revolutions in Europe	
Californian Gold Rush began	
The Spiritualist movement began in New York State	
Karl Marx and Fredrick Engels published *The Communist Manifesto*	
1848 (to 1850) A cholera epidemic claimed 52,000 lives	**1848** Public Health Act

Socio-Cultural Timeline	Monarchy, State and Church	

has been published annually since its inception.

Approximately 700 people were evicted from their crofts on North Uist by Lord Macdonald in a Highland Clearance.

1850	**1850**	**1850**
The first emigrants arrived in New Zealand	Irish Franchise Act increased the rural electorate	Civil registration began on Alderney.
The first census in the United States, to name all household members		

1851

1850

Civil registration began on Alderney.

1851
The Great Exhibition attracted millions of visitors

Australian Gold rush began

Population, 27.5 million

First Canadian census held

Winchester was the first English town to open a public library

1851
Catholic dioceses of Westminster and Southwark were founded

1851

Sunday, 30 March. A national census was undertaken, requiring more detailed information. Namely the relationship of each person to the head of the household and whether anyone was deaf or blind.

Information on the place of birth is also recorded. This census was the first to record the numbers of persons living on vessels, in inland waters or at sea, those serving abroad (with the armed forces or with the East India Company) and also those resident overseas. For Ireland only the returns for Fermanagh and Antrim survive.

The 'Religious Census' was held on 30 March amid much controversy. All places of worship across England, Wales and Scotland were recorded with a view to finding out the extent of religious instruction.

Although reports, made by ministers, were not compulsory, thousands were returned. The Scottish report lacked detail but the report for England and Wales was full of information and was published in 1854.

1851 (to 1875)

Henceforth, fathers' names could not be recorded on a birth certificate if the parents were not married.

1851 (to 1924)

The Empty House Tax (*aka* House Duty) was imposed after the repeal of the Window Tax.

1852

Civil registration districts re-organised.

A Burials Act permitted local authorities to open cemeteries to relieve the overcrowding of churchyards.

1853

A Succession Duty was introduced in connection with death duties as tax was now payable on the legal transfer of a dead person's assets.

Socio-Cultural Timeline	Monarchy, State and Church
1852 The first purpose-built music hall opened in Lambeth	**1852 (to 1852)** Earl of Derby, Edward Stanley, Conservative
Floods in Holmfirth, West Yorkshire, left many dead	**1852 (to 1855)** Earl of Aberdeen, George Hamilton- Gordon, Conservative
1853 (to 1854) London cholera epidemic killed more than 10,000 people	

Socio-Cultural Timeline	Monarchy, State and Church	

1853 (to 1923)

Records for Naval Ratings began giving details of birth, physical appearance, occupation and ships upon which they served. (TNA)

1853 (until 1948)

Vaccination against smallpox, administered through workhouses, was now compulsory. Registers of those vaccinated were kept from 1862.

1854 (to 1929)
The Orphan Train Movement operated in North America, moving destitute children from cities to rural areas

1854
Great Fire of Newcastle and Gateshead

1854 (to 1856)
Crimean War. Britain would lose more than 25,000 men

The Charge of the Light Brigade

1854 (to 1975)

The Lands Valuation (Scotland) Act established assessors offices in each Scottish county and royal burgh whose task it was to produce lists of properties above a certain value. The returns, which were often very detailed with information for example on tenants or other occupiers, have been digitised and are available online via NAS.

1855 (to 1858)
Viscount Palmerston, Henry Temple, Liberal

1855

Civil Registration began in Scotland.

1856
Van Diemen's Land renamed Tasmania

1856
County and Borough Police Act required the compulsory establishment of county forces

Many regional newspapers were founded as stamp duty on newspapers was abolished.

1857
First Victoria Cross awarded

1857
After the Indian Rebellion, the East India Company

1857

The Court of Probate Act moved responsibility for the granting of probate and letters of administration from the church courts to a new civil court and created the Principal Probate registry in London and several district probate registries.

The Matrimonial Causes Act permitted divorce in England and Wales on grounds of adultery by the wife or, in some cases, of adultery by the husband. The Act gave women who were living apart from their husbands control over money from bequests and investments and other earnings. It came into force on 1 January 1858, except in Ireland where a private parliamentary act was required. Jurisdiction over matrimonial issues passed from the church to civil courts.

A Parliamentary act gave magistrates powers to send homeless children to Industrial Schools.

1858

English, Welsh and Irish wills, previously granted by the Principal Probate Registries in London and Dublin, via local probate officers. Wills and administrations are indexed separately.

Crockford's Clerical Directory began and contains brief biographical details of Anglican clergy in Britain.

Socio-Cultural Timeline

Cartes de visite (patented in 1854) were introduced to England, a photographic format that remained popular until the early 1900s

1858
The Great Stink in London gave rise to the construction of the sewers

First case of diphtheria recorded

Monarchy, State and Church

passed control to the British government (the Raj lasted from 1858-1947)

Ottawa proclaimed the capital of Canada

1858 (to 1859)
Earl of Derby, Edward Stanley, Conservative

Socio-Cultural Timeline	Monarchy, State and Church	

1859
Diphtheria epidemic

The Great Storm wrecked 200 ships around the British coast including a steamship off Anglesey with the loss of more than 450 lives (The Anglesey Ship Disaster)

Charles Darwin's *On the Origin of Species* was published

1860s
Mechanised mower and reapers began to replace the traditional sickle and scythe

1860
The Criminal Lunatic Asylums Act proposed a system of dedicated asylums

1860-61
Unification of Italy

1861
Population, 29 million

In Russia, Alexander II emancipated serfs

1861 (to 1865)
American Civil War

1859 (to 1865)
Viscount Palmerston, Henry Temple, Liberal

1861
Death penalty abolished for all crimes except murder, high treason, piracy with violence and arson in the royal dockyards

1859

Medical registers began. (Registers to 1959 are available to search online)

1860s

There was now compliance in the registration of births and deaths on Guernsey, Herm and Jethou.

1860

Francis Frith began his project to photograph every town and village across Britain.

1861

Sunday, 7 April. National census, using the format that had been adopted in 1851.

American Civil War led to a blockade of cotton exports with devastating effect on the English textile industry, leading to riots in the spring of 1863.

Socio-Cultural Timeline	↑	Monarchy, State and Church
		1861 Prince Albert died of typhus
1862 Last recorded slaving voyage left from Liverpool		
1863 The first urban underground railway line in the world opened between Paddington and Farringdon In the US, the Confederates were defeated at the Battle of Gettysburg		**1863** Public Works Act
1864 The Sheffield Flood left 270 dead		
1865 A Welsh settlement began in Argentina In the mid 1860s, the cabinet card began to displace *cartes de visite*		**1865 (to 1866)** Earl Russell, John Russell, Liberal

1862

The Land Registry Act was passed in an effort to record the conveyance of land in the UK. Further acts in 1875 and 1897 improved the system until it was overhauled in 1925.

1864

Civil registration of all births, marriages and deaths began in Ireland.

1865

The Salvation Army was founded by William and Catherine Booth as the East London Christian Mission. It was founded in Wales in 1874 and in Jersey and Scotland in 1879.

William Lawrence began his project to photograph the towns and villages of Ireland. The complete collection is available online.

Record of Title Act was passed for Ireland to regulate the recording of land conveyance. The records can be accessed online by the public for a fee.

Socio-Cultural Timeline	Monarchy, State and Church
1866 In London's East End, a cholera epidemic killed 5,500	**1866 (to 1868)** Earl of Derby, Edward Stanley, Conservative
The Great Gale of Brixham killed many and destroyed the fishing fleet	**1866** The Isle of Man granted a measure of home rule
Oaks Colliery disaster killed almost 400 miners and rescuers	
1867 The Singer Company opened a factory in Glasgow producing sewing machines for the UK market	**1867** Canada became a self-governing dominion in the British Commonwealth
	Fenian rising in Ireland
	Suffrage groups began to be established across Britain
1868 Abolition of public executions	

1866

Age of the deceased was now added to the death index.

Agricultural Returns began to be collected. Later called Parish Summaries. A few late 18th and early 19th century returns were made; all originals have been destroyed but copies can be found in TNA.

1867

The Second Reform Act enfranchised the male town dwellers and widened eligibility amongst men who lived in rural areas in England and Wales, doubling the numbers entitled to vote to about 2 million. A similar act passed in Scotland the following year doubled the number of voters to about 230,000.

The Agricultural Gangs Act (covering England and Wales) was passed to regulate the employment of women and children and to ensure that gang masters were licensed.

Diamonds discovered in central South Africa led to the departure of many British migrants.

1868

In Scotland, the age at death was added to the statutory death index.

It was now possible to stipulate inheritance of real estate in a will. Previously this was governed by strict rules of descent.

Transportation of convicts to Australia ends.

Collection of church rates abolished by an act of parliament.

1868 (to 1868)
Benjamin Disraeli, Conservative

1868 (to 1874)
William Ewart Gladstone, Liberal

1869

Female rate-payers (single or widowed) could now vote in municipal elections, for Poor Law boards and (from 1870) for school boards. The qualifying residency period for all municipal voters was reduced to one year.

The completion of the Suez Canal led to a strong British presence in Egypt, Sudan and East Africa.

1869 (to 1948)

The Lloyd's Captains' Registers began recording details of careers. (LMA)

1869
The Debtor's Act ended imprisonment for debt

Great Fire of Whitstable drew thousands of sightseers and devastated the town

1869
Church of Ireland dis-established as the state church

1870

Married Women's Property Act gave married women in England, Wales and Ireland the right to keep their own earnings, and property inherited after marriage (see also 1882). Women were now admitted into Oxford and Cambridge Universities.

Dr Thomas Barnardo opened his first home for orphaned children in Stepney.

1870
Agricultural depression began – land values dropped and many bankruptcies amongst farmers

Horse-drawn trams introduced to London

1870
Army Enlistment (Short Service) Act allowed for shorter service period

Naturalisation Act. Applicants required to have served the Crown or to have lived in Britain for at least five years before they could be considered

Socio-Cultural Timeline	Monarchy, State and Church

Plain postcards began to be issued by the Post Office

Forster's Education Act provided elementary education for children of 5 to 12 years.

1870-71
Franco-Prussian War led many French to find temporary refuge in England

Teachers were required to keep attendance lists and log books of events on a weekly basis.

Gladstone introduced an Irish Land Act to reform injustices with regard to land ownership in Ireland. Further and more effective acts were passed in the 1880s.

In England and Wales, wills and probate administration were now indexed together.

1871
Bank Holidays were introduced for bank workers and were soon widely adopted

The Great Gale struck the north east coast of England

Population, 31.6 million

Guncotton factory explosion, Stowmarket

Proclamation of German empire

1871
Regulation of the Forces Act (Cardwell Reforms), created a structure of regional Brigade (Regimental) Districts

1871

Sunday, 2 April. A national census was conducted which continued the earlier format but added a further question concerning whether any member of the household was an 'imbecile or idiot' or 'feeble-minded'. This question was not asked from 1911 onwards. Individuals were also asked about their employment status

Trade Unions were now legalised.

Military pensions introduced.

1872
First ever Football Association (FA) Cup Final at Kennington Oval in London

1872

Secret ballot introduced for all elections in Britain and Ireland. Poll books showing voting records discontinued.

1872 (until 1939)

Barnardo began to send children to Canada through Miss Annie Macpherson's organisation. This was known as the British Home Children Scheme.

1873

In England and Wales the Returns of the Owners of Land published naming those with more than one acre. These were organised by county with landowners' addresses, land holdings and gross rental value. A revised and corrected edition was published in 1883.

1874

A Factory Act introduced a 56-hour week.

The Births and Deaths Registration Act made registration compulsory. Registration of a birth was now the responsibility of a baby's parents or the occupier of the house where a birth took place. Registration had to take place within 42 days else a fine of £2 was payable. The date of birth was sometimes altered by parents who failed to register within the specified time limit.

Responsibility for recording a death now fell to a relative of the deceased. Registration had to be made within

Socio-Cultural Timeline	Monarchy, State and Church
1873 (until 1877) The Panic of 1873 ushers in economic depression across Europe and North America	**1873** Royal Naval Hospital, Greenwich established The age of sail ended with the commissioning of HMS *Devastation*, a steam driven Royal Navy warship
1874 Massive storms hit the Yorkshire coast Astley Deep Pit Disaster	**1874 (to 1880)** Benjamin Disraeli, Conservative

Socio-Cultural Timeline	Monarchy, State and Church

five days of death and the cause of death was now to be certified by a doctor before a certificate could be issued. Burial authorities now required official notification regarding the registration of a death in order to prevent unauthorised interment.

1875

1875

The Public Health Act enabled local authorities to make by-laws regulating the building of new housing

The practice of using children to sweep chimneys began to cease with the Chimney Sweepers Act

The Artisans and Labourers Dwellings Improvement Act passed allowing local councils to purchase, demolish and replace slum housing. In Birmingham, some slum areas were rebuilt, though relatively few councils acted until later in the century.

Some Church of Ireland registers sent to the PRO in Dublin (marriage registers dating from before 1845 and baptisms and burial registers from 1871). About 60 per cent were deposited.

The Registration of Births and Deaths Act of 1874 came into effect and made the registration of a birth compulsory. It was now the responsibility of the parents or the householder where a birth occurred. The father of an illegitimate child had now to be present at registration in order for his name to be added to the records.

1876 (until 1936)

In Scotland, an annual list began to be made of testaments (wills) known as the *Calendar of Confirmations and Inventories*. (They can be searched online).

In Ireland, the *Returns of the Owners of Land* was published, organised by county with landowners' addresses, land holdings and gross rental value.

1878

Civil registration of births and deaths now compulsory on the Isle of Man.

Electoral registers began to show both Parliamentary and municipal voters as a result of a Registration Act.

A Factory and Workshop Act consolidated previous legislation and applied it to all trades. The minimum working age was raised to 10 years. Children below the age of 10 were required to attend school. Subsequent acts refined, amended and extended the provisions including raising the minimum employment age to 11 from 1891 and to 12 in 1901.

1879

The Irish Land League was established as a political organization,

Socio-Cultural Timeline	Monarchy, State and Church
1876 Alexander Graham Bell patented the telephone	**1876** Royal Titles Act – Queen Victoria proclaimed Empress of India
Native American sovereignty over the West began to decline after the Battle of Little Bighorn in the US	**1877** Britain annexed the Transvaal
1877 The Knowlton Trial and the formation of the Malthusian League	**1878** Royal Navy frigate HMS *Eurydice* capsized off the Isle of Wight with the loss of over 300 men
1878 The paddle steamer SS *Princess Alice* sank in the Thames leaving 700 dead	
Alexander Graham Bell demonstrates the telephone to Queen Victoria	
1879 Mosley Street in Liverpool was the first public road lit by electric light	

set up to help poor tenant farmers find ways of owning the land they worked.

Socio-Cultural Timeline	Monarchy, State and Church
1879 A public telephone service introduced in Britain Tay Bridge disaster	**1879** British defeated the Zulus in Natal
1880 The University of London began to award women their degrees	**1880** Greenwich Mean Time (GMT) adopted across Great Britain
	1880 (to 1881) First Anglo-Boer War
	1880 (to 1885) William Ewart Gladstone, Liberal
1881 (to 1884) Many thousands of Jews fled pogroms in Russia and came to England	
1881 Scotland's worst fishing disaster claimed 189 lives Population, 35 million	

1880

The Elementary Education Act made schooling compulsory for children from 5-10 years of age. Children of 13 years and under, who were in work, had to have a certificate to demonstrate that they had reached a certain standard.

The Burial Laws Amendment Act permitted the interment of any who were entitled to burial in a parochial burial place, provided the church incumbent was informed. A religious service was no longer required. The Act also permitted the use of a Church of England service on unconsecrated ground.

First British telephone directory published.

1881

Sunday, 3 April. A national census was undertaken using the pattern established in 1871. In Scotland, enumerators were required to ask if Gaelic was spoken at home.

Army regiments changed to territorial titles.

	Socio-Cultural Timeline	Monarchy, State and Church

1882

Married Women's Property Act gave married women in England, Wales and Ireland the same rights as single women to control all of their financial affairs, including ownership of property, running a business, being liable for debts and making wills. Scottish acts of 1877, 1880 and 1881 improved women's control of their finances and property, but less so than in the rest of the UK.

1882
Militant Irish Republicans killed Lord Frederick Cavendish and Thomas Henry Burke in Phoenix Park, Dublin

1883
More than 180 children died in the Sunderland theatre disaster

Boys Brigade founded

1884

Civil Registration for marriages on the Isle of Man made compulsory. Probate was transferred from church courts to the Manx High Court of Justice.

The Third Reform Act gave the vote in Parliamentary elections to most male householders in the countryside.

1884
The Fabian Society was founded in London

1884 (to 1885)
The Berlin Conference divided Africa among European colonial powers

1884 (to 1943)

Reports of suitability of naval officers for promotion.

1885

The cremation of the dead was legalized and the first crematorium in Britain opened in Woking, Surrey.

The Salvation Army established a Family Tracing Service in an attempt to reunite family members.

1885 (to 1886)
Marquess of Salisbury, Robert A T Gascoyne-Cecil, Conservative

Socio-Cultural Timeline	Monarchy, State and Church
1886 Gold rush in Transvaal	**1886 (to 1887)** William Ewart Gladstone, Liberal
1887 Widespread celebrations marked Queen Victoria's Golden Jubilee. These included an American Exhibition in London which featured Buffalo Bill and his Wild West Show	**1887 (to 1892)** Marquess of Salisbury, Robert A.T. Gascoyne-Cecil, Conservative
1888 The first Kodak camera Jack the Ripper murders began in Whitechapel The start of professional football	
1889 First moving pictures developed on celluloid film Prevention of Cruelty to, and Protection of, Children Act	**1889** First Official Secrets Act

1888

A Local Government Act established county councils and boroughs in England and Wales; effective early 1889, abolished 1974. A similar Scottish Act came into force in 1880.

County Electors Act was introduced so that now individuals who paid rates or occupied property with a rental value of more than £10 qualified for the vote in county and borough elections. Women qualified on the same basis if they were rate-payers or occupiers in their own right.

1889

Charles Booth began his detailed survey of the London poor (https://booth.lse.ac.uk/). The survey was made by Booth and his assistants walking the London streets and reporting on the state of housing and living conditions in each one. Booth produced a map to accompany the report which was later published as *Life and Labour of the People*.

1891

Sunday, 5 April. A national census using the established format was held, though the question regarding employment status was removed until 1931. Instead, individuals were asked if they were an employer or employee. In Wales, enumerators asked individuals what languages were spoken in the home.

1892

The Foreign Marriage Act granted validation to certain marriages that occurred abroad where one of the parties was a British subject.

1893

Elementary Education (School Attendance) Act raised the school leaving age to 11 and later, in 1899, to 12 years of age. A further act made education compulsory for children who were deaf or blind. Provision was made for special schools to be established.

1894

Royal Mail permits publishers in Britain to make and distribute picture postcards.

Socio-Cultural Timeline	Monarchy, State and Church
1891 Population, 37.8 million The Great Blizzard – 200 lives lost	
1891-2 Buffalo Bill's Wild West Show toured England	**1892** British troops inflicted heavy casualties in their conquest of Ijebu-Ode in modern-day Nigeria
	1893 Independent Labour Party founded in Bradford
	1894 (to 1895) Earl of Rosebery, Liberal

Socio-Cultural Timeline	Monarchy, State and Church	
		Estate Duty was introduced whereby a tax was levied on assets owned by a person at death.
		The Local Government Act established Urban and Rural District Councils and Parish Councils elected by rate-payers.
	1895 (to 1902) Marquess of Salisbury, Robert A T Gascoyne-Cecil, Conservative	**1895** Notification of infectious diseases became compulsory.
1896 The wireless telegraph invented by Marconi was first used in England. Underground Railway opened in Glasgow	**1897** Suffrage groups joined to form the National Union of Women's Suffrage Societies led by Millicent Fawcett	The *Dictionary of National Biography* first published. **1898** Catholic priests could now perform legally binding marriages and non-conformist congregations could nominate a member of their church as a registrar of marriages. Local Government Act (Ireland) formed county councils. The value of total estate was now shown in the probate indexes of England and Wales.
	1899 (to 1902) Second Anglo-Boer War. Losses of soldiers during Black Week (10 to 17 December 1899) led to the recruitment of an additional 180,000 men	**1899** The very informative and illustrated *Victoria County History* series began with detailed commentaries on each county, discussion of buildings of historical note and much of interest to the genealogist.

Chapter Ten

1900s

	Socio-Cultural Timeline	Monarchy, State and Church
1900 Higher elementary schools were recognized, providing education from the age of 10 to 15 years of age. One in six of the population of England and Wales were employed 'in service'.	**1900** The lifting of the Siege of Mafeking in May generated celebrations across Britain Labour Party formed	
1901 Sunday, 31 March. A national census was held. A question was added to the established format, enquiring if individuals worked at home. Returns are complete for Ireland. Many men were engaged in the 2nd Anglo-Boer War and so are not included in the census data.	**1901** Marconi transmitted the first radio wave Population, 41.6 million	**1901** House of Saxe-Coburg and Gotha **1901 (to 1910)** Edward VII
1902 Provision for secondary education through Balfour's Education Act.	**1902 (until 1904)** Buffalo Bill's Wild West Show toured England	**1902 (to 1905)** Arthur Balfour, Conservative
1903 In Ireland, the mother's maiden name was now added to the birth index.	**1903** First aeroplane flight A popular folding camera was introduced by Kodak	**1903** In Manchester Emmeline Pankhurst founded the Women's Social and Political Union, a suffragette movement that advocated militant tactics to gain women the vote

Socio-Cultural Timeline	Monarchy, State and Church
1905 Albert Einstein published his theory of relativity	**1905 (to 1908)** Sir Henry Campbell-Bannerman, Liberal
1907 Scouts Movement founded	
New Zealand became self-governing within the British Empire	
1908 London Olympics	**1908 (to 1916)** Herbert H. Asquith, Liberal (1915 Coalition)
Mass production began in the US of the Model T Ford	**1908** Territorial Army force created

1905

An Aliens' Act introduced registration of immigrants and restrictions on those who came to settle in Britain. The act was designed to prevent destitute individuals or criminals entering the country.

1906

Inheritance Tax introduced.

The Marriage with Foreigners Act meant that notice had to be given to a local superintendent registrar for some (but not all) marriages that took place abroad.

1907

Midwives (or parents of a child) were now required to notify the local health ministry of births to prevent missed registration.

The Deceased Wife's Sister's Marriage Act allowed a man to marry his dead wife's sister.

1908

The Children Act introduced regulations concerning baby farming and wet nursing and led to the establishment of juvenile courts and many orphanages.

Socio-Cultural Timeline	Monarchy, State and Church

1909

Old Age Pensions introduced by Lloyd George, which helped to alleviate the fear of entering a workhouse.

1909
Rail and coal strikes

Extreme weather caused the Isle of Man paddle steamer *Ellan Vannin*, to sink en route to Liverpool

1910 (to 1915)

A survey of land ownership in England and Wales, sometimes called Lloyd George's Doomsday, was carried out in support of The Finance Act.

1910
Girl Guides founded

Westhoughton Pit Disaster killed almost 350 men and boys

Formation of the Union of South Africa Act by former colonies of Cape Colony, Natal, Transvaal and Orange Free State

1910 (to 1936)
George V

1910 (until 1911)
First Tonypandy (Rhonda) riots by miners

1911

Sunday, 2 April. A National Census known as the 'fertility census' was boycotted by the suffragist Women's Freedom League. Irish returns complete.

The National Insurance Act gave sickness benefits to working people and access to a doctor.

1911
Sidney Street Siege

Population, 42.1 million

Socio-Cultural Timeline	Monarchy, State and Church

Mother's maiden names added to England and Wales GRO birth indexes.

The Society of Genealogists established.

Unemployment benefits introduced.

1912
RMS *Titanic* sank

First British cinema opened in Clevedon, Somerset

1912

A spouse's surname was added to the GRO marriage indexes in England and Wales.

1913
Suffragette demonstrations in London

In South Wales, the Senghenydd pit disaster claimed the lives of 439 miners

The first county record office opened in Bedford

1913

The first child migrants in modern times arrived in Western Australia, bound for the Fairbridge School at Pinjarra in Western Australia. As many as 130,000 children were subsequently taken to colonial outposts until the migrant scheme stopped in 1970.

1914
German raid on Scarborough and Hartlepool

RMS *Empress of Ireland* sank with a crew mostly from Merseyside

1914
Irish Home Rule Act

First World War began

Battle of Ypres

Battle of Loos

1914

Notice of official name changes by deed poll now published in *The London Gazette*.

British Nationality and Status of Aliens Act – all aliens over 16 to register with police.

1915
First Zeppelin raid on Great Britain

1915
Evacuations from Gallipoli

1915
Civil registration introduced on Sark. National registration was introduced

	Socio-Cultural Timeline	Monarchy, State and Church

as a wartime measure and was administered by the General Register Office.

| | *Lusitania* sank claiming 1,200 lives | |
| | Quintinshill rail crash was Britain's worst rail accident | |

1916 (to 1919)

27 January 1916. Military Service Act imposed conscription on all single men aged between 18 and 41. The medically unfit, clergymen, teachers and certain classes of industrial worker were exempt.

	1916 Faversham munitions factory explosion claimed 100 lives	**1916** Easter Rising, armed rebellion in Ireland
	1917 Russian revolution	**1916 (to 1922)** David Lloyd George, Liberal (Coalition)
	First successful heavy bomber raid on London	Third Battle of Ypres (aka Passchendaele)
	USA joined the war	**1917 (to present)** King George V decreed that the royal surname was now Windsor

1918

The Representation of the People Act (or Fourth Reform Act) gave votes to men over 21 years of age and to women over 30 who were householders or wives of householders. The format of electoral registers also changed.

A parliamentary act made secondary education compulsory for all up to 14 years of age.

| | **1918 (to 1919)** Spanish Flu pandemic, claimed 228,000 lives in Britain | **1918** The Royal Flying Corps and the Royal Naval Air Service merged to form the Royal Air Force |
| | | **1918** 11 November, Armistice. End of First World War |

1919

Soldiers discharged from First World War service.

Registration of marriage began in Guernsey, Alderney and Sark.

| | **1919** Britain adopted a 48-hour working week | **1919** Treaty of Versailles |

Socio-Cultural Timeline	Monarchy, State and Church

Sinking of HMS *Iolaire* off Stornoway

1920s

British control of East Africa strengthened with significant colonial settlement until 1939.

1920

Census Act provided for a mid-term census and importantly included a statutory 100 year prohibition on disclosure.

Oxford University began to admit women to study for degrees.

1921
Population, 44 million

Marie Stopes opened the first permanent birth control clinic in Holloway, North London

1921

Sunday, 19 June. National Census.

1922
The beginnings of the British Broadcasting Corporation (BBC)

First public radio broadcasts in the UK

1922
Formation of the Irish Free State and Northern Ireland

1922 (to 1923)
Andrew Bonar Law, Conservative

1922

A sustained IRA attack at the end of June on the Four Courts in Dublin, which housed the GRO and the PRO, resulted in the destruction of many Protestant parish records, most poll books, wills, and almost all census returns from 1821-51. Complete census returns survive for 1901 and 1911 and a few fragments for 1821, 1831, 1841 and 1851. Census returns from 1861-91 had been pulped during WW1. The indexes for pre-1858 wills and the copies of will transcripts made thereafter and held in other places, were not affected.

The BMD registers for Northern Ireland and the Republic of Ireland were now kept separately.

The Law of Property Act brought an end to the manorial system with the final change of copyhold to freehold land taking place in 1926.

1923

Women were given the same divorce rights as men if adultery could be proved.

1923 (until 1967)

The first Barnardo's child migrants arrived in New South Wales, Australia.

1924

The Big Brother Movement founded to encourage young Britons to emigrate to Australia.

1925

Mothers were given custodial rights over children.

The Land Registration Act introduced a system which remains in use.

Registration of births and deaths begins in Alderney and Sark.

Socio-Cultural Timeline	Monarchy, State and Church
	1922 The Infanticide Act abolished the death penalty for women who killed their babies whilst suffering mental illness as a result of childbirth
1923 Founding of the English Place-Name Society	**1923 (to 1924)** Stanley Baldwin, Conservative
1924 Bristol Archives was the first borough record office to open in the UK	**1924 (to 1924)** James Ramsey MacDonald, Labour
	1924 (to 1929) Stanley Baldwin, Conservative
1925 John Logie Baird publicly demonstrated television	

Socio-Cultural Timeline	Monarchy, State and Church

1926
General Strike

1926

Births and Deaths Registration Act introduced the need for a legal proof (registrar's certificate or coroner's order) before a burial or cremation could take place. Notice also had to be made to a registrar once a funeral had occurred.

The act also made the registration of stillborn babies mandatory (in order to counteract infanticide). This took effect from 1 July 1927 though no national indexes are available.

A widow's entitlement to an intestate husband's estate increased from one third to one half. The remainder was to pass to children.

Adoption of Children Act came into effect in January 1927.

The Legitimacy Act permitted the offspring of unmarried parents to be legitimised provided the parents had been free to marry when their child was born.

1928
Alexander Fleming discovered penicillin and the revolution of antibiotics began

1928

Women over 21 years of age received the right to vote.

1929
US stockmarket crash, worldwide economic depression, mass

1929 (to 1935)
Ramsay MacDonald, Labour

1929

The age of consent (the minimum age for marriage to take place) was raised to 16 with parental consent by the Act of Marriage Act. It was previously variable, though generally held at 14 for boys and 12 for girls.

In Scotland, a mother's maiden name was added to the birth index.

Workhouses were abolished under the Local Government Act of 1929 though many were renamed Public Assistance Institutions and continued to function under the control of local councils.

1931

Sunday, 26 April. National Census. A question regarding employment status was re-introduced. All records for the 1931 census in England and Wales were destroyed in an accidental fire at Hayes, in Middlesex in 1942.

1933

Refugees from Nazi Germany began to arrive: some in transit for the US; many settled in the UK.

Socio-Cultural Timeline	Monarchy, State and Church
unemployment and poverty	
1930s Jews fleeing persecution in Europe arrived in Britain	
1930 One-fifth of the British male workforce was unemployed Clyde Tombaugh discovered Pluto	
1931 Population, 46 million	**1931** Death sentence for pregnant women abolished
1932 The National Hunger March began in Scotland	Statute of Westminster gave legal status to the independence of Canada, Australia, the Irish Free State, New Zealand, South Africa and Newfoundland
1934 Gresford Pit Disaster	**1934** South Africa became a fully sovereign nation state within the British Empire
	1935 (to 1937) Stanley Baldwin, Conservative

Socio-Cultural Timeline	Monarchy, State and Church
1936 Spanish Civil War began drawing many British to fight for the Republican cause	**1936 (January to December) Edward VIII**
Battle of Cable Street, London	**1936 (to 1952) George VI**
Jarrow March	
	1937 (to 1940) Neville Chamberlain, Conservative

1937

4,000 Basque children were brought to England to escape the dangers of the Spanish Civil War.

Matrimonial Causes Act broadened the grounds of divorce, this was extended to Northern Ireland in 1939.

Mass Observation began (until early 1950s and later revived in 1991), records in Sussex University and online (www.massobs.org.uk).

1938

Population Act allowed for the collation of birth registrations.

Arrival of the first Kindertransport, as young Jewish children were evacuated from Germany. The scheme continued until the outbreak of war in September 1939. 10,000 children were brought to safety. Many stayed permanently.

1939

Friday, 29 September. A mini census was held so that everyone could be issued with an identity card.

Evacuation of women and children from London began.

1939 (to 1960)

Compulsory military National Service. Formalised by the National Service Act 1948.

1940

September to May 1941 – the Blitz resulted in thousands of civilian deaths and destruction of records, including military records.

Socio-Cultural Timeline	Monarchy, State and Church
1939 Many Poles fled to England	**1939** Britain (and France) declared war on Germany. Operation Pied Piper began
	1940 (to 1945) Winston Churchill, Conservative
	Jersey and Alderney occupied by the Germans
	1940 Dunkirk evacuations
	Battle of Britain
	Alderney's population evacuated
	Blitz over Swansea
	Special Air Service formed
	First Canadian soldiers arrived in UK
	Operation Barbarossa: German invasion of Russia

Socio-Cultural Timeline	Monarchy, State and Church	

1941
Population,
48.2 million

1941

National Census – no census was held in 1941 because of the Second World War.

America joined the war and there were thousands of liaisons between US servicemen and British women. As many as 100,000 'GI babies' were born and as many marriages took place as women went to America after the war.

1942
Battle of El Alamein

First American soldiers arrived in the UK

Baedeker raids: Exeter, Bath, Norwich, York and Canterbury

1942

The bombing of Exeter resulted in the loss of almost all pre-1858 wills for Somerset, Devon and Cornwall. Some pre-existing abstracts and copies survive.

1943
Dam Buster raids

1943

The two year National Farm Survey concluded. (TNA)

1944
D-Day landings on Normandy beaches

1944

The Education (or Butler) Act established the tripartite education system of grammar schools, secondary modern schools and secondary technical schools.

1945
8 May, Victory in Europe Day

1945 (to 1951)
Clement Attlee, Labour

1945

The NRA was established to collect information about manuscripts outside public records.

1945 (to 1972)

The Australian government began to encourage British citizens to emigrate under an assisted passage scheme.

1946

Family Census carried out by the Registrar General on behalf of the Royal Commission on Population.

Civil registration districts reorganised.

1947

Polish Resettlement Act offered citizenship to over 200,000 displaced Polish troops in Britain.

The Royal Military Academy Sandhurst opens.

1948

The British Nationality Act created the new status of Citizen of the United Kingdom and the Colonies. All Commonwealth citizens now qualified for British passports. Thereafter many thousands came to Britain in search of work.

The Poor Law abolished by parliamentary act.

Socio-Cultural Timeline	Monarchy, State and Church
1945 15 August, Victory in Japan Day Atomic bombing of Hiroshima and Nagasaki George Orwell's *Animal Farm*	
1946 27 new towns including Harlow, Bracknell and Milton Keynes were built following the New Towns Act	
1947 Very harsh winter Education was now compulsory to 15 years of age	**1947** End of Raj as British rule of India came to an end
1947 (until 1991) Tensions between Russia and the US inaugurate the Cold War	
1948 National Health Service introduced Summer Olympics in London	

Socio-Cultural Timeline	↑	Monarchy, State and Church

Empire Windrush brought almost 500 passengers from colonies including Jamaica, many of whom came to England to help fill the post war labour shortage

Policy of apartheid adopted in South Africa

1949
Formation of NATO

1949

In Guernsey, married womens' deaths were now recorded under their married name. Previously the record had been under a woman's maiden name.

In Jersey probate jurisdiction was transferred from the Ecclesiastical Court of the Dean of Jersey to the Principal Probate Registry in London.

1951
Population, 50.2 million

1951 (to 1955)
Winston Churchill, Conservative

1951

Sunday, 8 April. National Census. The first full census since 1921 due to the war.

1951 (to 1953)

British troops were involved in the Korean War. Almost 700 would die; more than 1,000 were prisoners of war.

1951 (to 1974)

The first volume of Nikolaus Pevsner's *The Buildings of England* was published

– detailed county surveys of all buildings of historical note across the country.

1952

February – national identity cards abolished.

1957

The Legitimacy Act extended legitimacy to children born to parents who had not been free to marry at the time of their birth but who later married.

The 'Bring out a Briton' scheme was initiated to encourage further migration from Britain to Australia.

1958

Public Records Act – 50 year rule, amended 1967.

Socio-Cultural Timeline	Monarchy, State and Church
	1952 (to present) **Elizabeth II**
1952 Great Smog of London. Many died of respiratory disease	
1953 North Sea Flood left more than 300 dead in England	**1955 (to 1957)** Sir Anthony Eden, Conservative
Hillary and Tenzing climbed Mount Everest	
1956 Hungarian revolution (many refugees came to Britain)	
1957 Publication of the Wolfenden report on homosexuality and prostitution	**1957 (to 1963)** Harold Macmillan, Conservative
Windscale Fire, Cumbria	
Foundation of European Economic Community (EEC)	

Socio-Cultural Timeline	Monarchy, State and Church

1959
Auchengeich pit disaster

1960

The Population Statistics Act required the compulsory notification of causes of stillbirths.

Surman's card index, with biographical details of Congregational ministers from the mid 17th Century until 1972, was given to Dr Williams' Library.

1961
First man in space

Institute of Heraldic and Genealogical Studies founded in Canterbury

Population, 52.8 million

The Berlin Wall was built

Republic of South Africa established

1961

Sunday, 23 April. National Census. Although census forms were hand-filled, data was laboriously entered into a computer for the first time. All households received the 'short' form with one in ten also receiving the 'long' form.

1962
Cuban Missile Crisis

1962-3
The Big Freeze

1962

Commonwealth Immigrants Act increased the residence period for Commonwealth citizens (plus British subjects and Irish citizens) applying for registration as citizens of the UK and its colonies from one year to five years thus making it harder to gain permanent status.

1963

A parliamentary act (which came into effect in 1965) abolished the County of London and replaced it with Greater London.

1966

A mini-census was held on 24 April, based on a 10 per cent sample of the population.

1967

A Public Record Act shortened the length of time records were closed to 30 years, except for census records which remain closed for 100 years. Further redefined by the Freedom of Information Act in 2000.

Socio-Cultural Timeline	Monarchy, State and Church
1963 Assassination of US President Kennedy	**1963 (to 1964)** Sir Alec Douglas-Home, Conservative
	1964 (to 1970) Harold Wilson, Labour
1965 Abolition of capital punishment The Race Relations Act banned discrimination in public places National Survey of Gypsies	
1966 The collapse of a colliery spoil tip at Aberfan killed 116 children and 28 adults	**1966** The Troubles began in Northern Ireland
1967 Sexual Offences Act legalised consensual homosexual acts between men of 21 and over. The Act only applied to England and Wales	
1968 Severe floods across England Assassination in US of civil rights leader, Martin Luther King Jr	

Socio-Cultural Timeline	Monarchy, State and Church
1969 Representation of the People Act extended the vote to women and men over 18 First man on the moon British troops deployed in Northern Ireland	
1970s After changes in immigration laws were made, many Bengali Muslims (Bangladeshi people) came to work and settle in the UK	**1970 (to 1974)** Edward Heath, Conservative
1971 Decimalisation saw the introduction of a new currency Population, 55.9 million Ibrox Football Stadium disaster	**1971** Courts Act brought an end to Quarter Sessions and Assizes and replaced them with a single Crown Court

1969

The format of birth and death registers and certificates changed. Spaces were now made for a child's surname and parent's place of birth.

A Divorce Reform Act was passed making it easier to divorce. This came into effect in 1971.

The Family Law Reform Act enabled illegitimate offspring to inherit if either parent died intestate.

In Scotland, England and Wales, the date of birth was added to GRO death indexes.

The age at majority was reduced from 21 to 18 years of age.

Some 80,000 Britons emigrated to Australia.

The requirement for parental consent on a marriage was reduced from 21 years of age to 18.

1971

Sunday, 25 April. National Census. Country of birth added and more detailed questions regarding occupation.

The Immigration Act permitted an individual the right of abode in the UK if they, their husband, parents or grandparents had a connection with the UK, Channel Islands or the Isle of Man.

1971 (to present)

Electoral Register (eligibility to vote) now available for all men and women over the age of 18.

1972

Local Government Act (England and Wales) transformed the county structure (from 1974) as boundaries were changed. Some counties (including Rutland) ceased to exist and new ones came into being. 179 registration districts were abolished and many others were re-named.

55,000 Ugandans of Asian origin were forced to flee to Britain, with many settling in towns in the Midlands.

Merger of the Congregational and Presbyterian churches in England and Wales to form the United Reformed Church.

The newly created OPCS absorbed the GRO.

1973

Fire at the National Personnel Records Center in America destroyed 16-18 million military personnel files –

Socio-Cultural Timeline	Monarchy, State and Church
	1972 30 January, Bloody Sunday
1973 Concorde crossed the Atlantic for the first time	**1973** Britain and Ireland joined EEC
Global energy crisis	**1974 (to 1976)** Harold Wilson, Labour

Socio-Cultural Timeline	Monarchy, State and Church	
		relevant to Second World War 'GI babies'.
		Burghs in Scotland replaced by regions and districts.
1974 Flixborough chemical plant explosion		**1974** A mother's maiden name was added to the Scottish GRO death indexes.
1975 Democracy restored in Spain. Growth of holidays abroad	**1975** Equal Pay Act and Sex Discrimination Act	**1975** The Children Act permitted an adopted person to apply for their birth certificate. The Capital Transfer tax replaced previous death duty taxes.
	1976 (to 1979) James Callaghan, Labour	**1976** Deaths exceeded live births in England and Wales for the first time since records began in 1837.
	1977 Nationwide celebrations marked Queen Elizabeth II's Silver Jubilee	**1977** The National Archives opened in Kew as an adjunct to the PRO.
	1978-9 Winter of Discontent	The Abandoned Children's Register was introduced to record all babies whose parents were not known. Previously these details were recorded at parish level.
	1979 SAS stormed Iranian Embassy Lord Mountbatten murdered by the IRA	

Socio-Cultural Timeline		Monarchy, State and Church
		1979 (to 1990) Margaret Thatcher, Conservative

1981

Sunday, 5 April. National census.

The British Nationality Act abolished the status of the Citizens of UK and Colonies Act.

1984

In England and Wales the GRO BMD registers were now arranged annually instead of quarterly.

1987

The legal distinctions between children born to married and unmarried parents were removed through the Family Law Reform Act.

1988

An Education Reform Act made wide-ranging changes, including the notion of competition, whereby schools were encouraged to compete for pupils.

1981
Riots across Britain

Population, 56.3 million

1982
Falklands War

1984 (to 1985)
Miners' Strike after the announcement of the closure of 20 coal pits

1985
Toxteth and Broadwater Farm riots

Bradford City Stadium Fire

1985
Anglo-Irish Agreement

1987
The Great Storm

1988
Lockerbie air disaster

1989
Piper Alpha oil rig disaster

Kegworth air disaster

Hillsborough Stadium disaster

Marchioness riverboat disaster

Socio-Cultural Timeline	Monarchy, State and Church
Fall of the Berlin Wall	
Anti-Communist revolutions across eastern Europe	
1989-90 Tim Berners-Lee developed the World Wide Web (internet)	
1990 Poll Tax riots	**1990 (to 1991)** First Gulf War
Nelson Mandela, leader of the African National Congress released from prison after 27 years	**1990 (to 1997)** John Major, Conservative
1991 Population, 57.8 million	
1992 Civil war in Yugoslavia. British involved in peacekeeping	**1993** European Union was established
1994 Channel Tunnel opened	**1994** First female priests were ordained in the Church of England

1990

A Poll Tax, or community charge, replaced domestic rates.

1991

Sunday, 21 April. National census. As many as 1 million went uncounted owing to fears that the government would use information to enforce a poll tax.

1994

Council areas replaced regions and districts in Scotland.

1995

From 1 April any suitable, privately owned premises could be licensed for marriage ceremonies. This led to an increasing trend for couples to marry away from their place of birth.

1996

OPCS became part of the new ONS.

1997
Widespread
mourning after the
death of Diana,
Princess of Wales

1997 (to 2007)
Tony Blair, Labour

1998
Good Friday
Agreement,
official end of
'The Troubles' in
Northern Ireland

Omagh Bomb

1999

Separate parliaments began in Wales,
Scotland and Northern Ireland.

The House of Lords Act brought an
end to inherited peerages.

Chapter Eleven

2000s

2000
Autumn brought the wettest weather across Britain since records began in 1766

2000

Countrywide celebrations to mark the Millenium

Freedom of Information Act – meant people could now access records; even ones closed under the 30 year rule.

2001
11 September, World Trade Centre attack (9/11) in New York

Population, 59 million

2001

Sunday, 29 April. National Census. Approximately 94 per cent of the population was recorded.

2002
Queen Elizabeth II's Golden Jubilee

2002

Nationality, Immigration and Asylum Act permitted children born to British mothers overseas registration as UK citizens.

The Land Registration Act brought further change to existing procedures of recording land conveyance. Details of land ownership can be accessed from Her Majesty's Land Registry.

Freedom of Information (Scotland) Act.

Socio-Cultural Timeline	Monarchy, State and Church

2003 (to 2010)

Second Gulf War

2003

TNA was created, combining the PRO with the HMC, HMSO and OPSI. Over 3 billion items from the TNA archives were published online by the UK government

2004

Enlargement of the EU led to many thousands of Poles and others from Eastern Europe coming to Britain.

New edition of the *Dictionary of National Biography* published.

2005

From 30 December it became legal to trace adopted people via an intermediary agency.

Same-sex civil partnerships introduced.

2007

First saliva-based DNA testing for Ancestry launched.

2010

Constitutional Reform and Governance Act reduced the 30-year rule to 20 years. Two years' worth of

2004
Only 13 coal mines remained open (compared to 169 in 1984)

2005
Terrorist attacks in London (7/7)

IRA declared an end to their armed struggle

2007 (to 2010)
Gordon Brown, Labour

2010 (to 2016)
David Cameron, Conservative
Nick Clegg, Liberal Democrat (Coalition government)

Socio-Cultural Timeline	Monarchy, State and Church
	2010 Bloody Sunday inquiry – army 'unjustified' in shooting 27 civilians in 1972
2011 Riots across Britain	
Population, 63.2 million	
News of the World closes	
2011 Claude Choules the last combat veteran of World War I died	
2012 Summer Olympics held in London	**2012** Queen Elizabeth II's Diamond Jubilee
	Welfare Reform Act – controversial changes to Incapacity Benefit and introduction of Bedroom Tax
	Richard III's body was discovered under a car park in Leicester
2013 Code breaker, Alan Turing given a posthumous royal pardon	**2013** General Synod of the Church of England voted for ordination of women bishops
Extensive flooding across England and Wales continues into the early months of 2014	

government records to be transferred to TNA and PRONI each year until 2022. Thereafter will be yearly.

2011

Sunday, 27 March. National census. Findings include: increase of people stating no religion, fall in home ownership and rise in rented accommodation, increased distances travelled to work, and only 1% of workers are in agriculture.

2013

The Freedom of Information (Scotland) Act 2002 (Historical Periods) Order 2013 reduces the period of time Scottish Government records become 'historical' from 30 years to 15 years.

	Socio-Cultural Timeline	Monarchy, State and Church

2014

TNA released records of over 12,000 servicemen from the Household Cavalry from 1799 to 1920 (WO 400).

Through its *First World War 100* web portal, TNA and IWM released a series of war diaries covering 1914 to 1922 (WO 95).

TNA added UK Government's social media platforms Twitter and YouTube to their web archive.

2014
First same-sex marriages permitted in England and Wales

2015

Records of local interest; eg Magistrates' courts, NHS, made available under the 20-year rule.

TNA released Royal Navy Ratings 'records of service' who served between 1924 and 1929 (ADM 362) and continuation cards for those who served after 1 January 1929 also available (ADM 363).

2015
London's population hits a record high of 8.6 million

2018
Measles was declared eradicated in the UK

The Human Genome Project completed by scientists in Cambridge

2019
The first opposite-sex couples were granted civil partnerships in England and Wales

2020
Covid-19 pandemic began

2015
Rachel Treweek, Bishop of Gloucester, first woman bishop in the House of Lords

2016
The UK voted to leave the European Union (Brexit)

2016 (to 2019)
Theresa May, Conservative

2017
Cressida Dick became the first female Commissioner of the Metropolitan Police in London

2019 (to present)
Boris Johnson, Conservative

Socio-Cultural Timeline	Monarchy, State and Church

2021

Sunday 21 March. National Census. For the first time predominantly online with a target of 75 per cent online return rate. Question changes included: sexual orientation, gender identification, ethnic grouping, supervisory status and armed forces service.

Subject Index

The subjects listed below cover most of the entries in the timeline. Search for the subject you require and you will see the relevant date or dates under which information may be found.

insanity & mental health, c.1407, 1774, 1808, 1845, 1860
Institute of Heraldic and Genealogical Studies, 1961
insurance records, 1710, 1782, 1911
internet, 1989-90
Ipswich, 1823
Ireland, 1171, 1535, 1542, 1582, 1586, 1600, 1611, 1634, 1651, 1653, 1655, 1657, 1659, 1679, 1695, 1708, 1730, 1740, 1766, 1776, 1778, 1791, 1796, 1798, 1800, 1814, 1821, 1823, 1829, 1831, 1836, 1837, 1838, 1841, 1845, 1847, 1848, 1850, 1851, 1864, 1865, 1867, 1869, 1870, 1872, 1875, 1879, 1895, 1898, 1903, 1914, 1917, 1922, 1966, 1972, 1973, 1985, 1999
  Act for the Settlement of Ireland, 1652
  Munster plantation, 1595, 1606
  Northern, 1922, 1939, 1966, 1969, 1998, 1999
  Ulster plantation, 1630, 1634, 1642, 1652, 1653, 1655, 1659, 1679, 1715
Ireton, Henry, 1661
Irish Republican Army (IRA), 1922
Isle of Man, 1079, 1266, 1399, 1405, 1511, 1706, 1765, 1849, 1866, 1878, 1884, 1909, 1971
Italy, 1860

Jack Cade's Rebellion, 1450
Jacobitism, 1689, 1715, 1719, 1740, 1746
Jamaica, 1655, 1948
Jamestown, Virginia, 1607
Jarrow March, 1936
Jersey, 1204, 1461, 1471, 1602, 1842, 1865, 1940, 1949
Jethou, 1840, 1860s
Jews, 1189–90, 1210, 1278, 1290, 1656, 1734, 1753, 1881, 1938–9
Jewish Naturalisation Act, 1753

Kabul, 1842
Kelly's Directories, 1845
Kent, 1576, 1709, 1788, 1801
Kett's Rebellion, 1549
Kilkenny, statutes of, 1366
Kindertransport, 1938
King's County, see Offaly
Knatchbull's Act, 1723
Knights Templar, 1119, 1185
Knowlton Trial, The, 1877

labourers, 1350, 1351, 1388
  Ordinance of, 1349
  Statute of, 1351
Lambeth, 1656
Lancashire, 1612
Lancaster, Duchy of, c.1272
land conveyance & valuation, 1617, 1634, 1862, 1865
land tenure & ownership, 1086, 1198, 1290, 1660, 1870, 1873, 1876, 1879, 1910
Land Registration Act, 1925, 2002
Land Registry, 1602, 1862 (Act)
Langland, William, 1377
Latin, 1733
Lay Subsidy Rolls, 1290
Leicester, 2012
Leland, John, 1539
Lewes, 1077
Liberate Rolls, 1226
Liber Feodorum, 1198
Licensing Act, The, 1753
Licensing Order, 1643
Lincoln cathedral, 1185
Lincolnshire, 1536
Lincoln's Inn, 1422
linen, 1796
Liverpool, 1699, 1715, 1799, 1830s, 1845, 1862, 1909
livery companies, 1155
Lloyd's Captains' Registers, 1869
Lloyd's Register of Shipping, 1764
local government, 1835, 1888, 1894, 1895, 1898, 1929, 1972, 1973, 1994
London, 1067, 1170, 1272, 1278, 1351, 1485, 1559, 1603, 1607, 1618, 1630s, 1653, 1677, 1691, 1695, 1717, 1734, 1740, 1741, 1750, 1753, 1764, 1772, 1780, 1795, 1799, 1823, 1840, 1853, 1858, 1866, 1872, 1889, 1917, 1921, 1936, 1963, 2005
  City Mission, 1835
  Great Fire of, 1666
  Great Plague of, 1665
  Great Smog, 1952
  Great Stink, 1858
  Johnstone's London Commercial Guide and Street Directory, 1817
  map of, 1747, 1792, 1827
  mayor of, 1290
  The Little London Directory, 1677
  Topography of London, 1810
  University, 1836, 1880

rotten borough, 1832
Rotuli de Dominabus et Pueris de XII Comitatibus, 1185
Rotuli Hundredorum, 1255
Royal Academy, The, 1768
Royal African Company, The, 1672, 1698
Royal Air Force, 1918
Royal Declaration of Indulgence, 1672
Royal Naval Hospital, 1873
Royal Society, The, 1660
Russia, 1555, 1703, 1861, 1881, 1941, 1985
Rutland, 1522, 1817, 1972

Saladin Tithe, 1188
Salford, 1772
Salisbury, 1685
Salvation Army, 1865, 1885
Sark, 1336, 1915, 1916, 1919, 1925
Saxton, Christopher, 1679
Scarborough, 1626, 1914
schools, *see* Education
Scilly naval disaster, 1707
Scone, 1651
Scotland, 1124, 1266, 1296, 1306, 1347, 1437, 1506, 1536, 1552, 1560, 1574, 1582, 1597, 1600, 1603, 1611, 1617, 1639, 1653, 1672, 1689, 1694, 1695, 1696, 1715, 1736, 1741, 1752, 1754, 1778, 1784, 1788, 1792, 1820s, 1800, 1824, 1830, 1845, 1846, 1851, 1854, 1855, 1865, 1867, 1868, 1876, 1881, 1882, 1929, 1969, 1973, 1994, 1999, 2002
A Description of the Western Isles, 1695
Settlement Act, The, 1662, 1687, 1697
Settlement Certificate, 1601, 1662, 1697
Shakespeare, William, 1616
Sheffield, 1864
Ships' Muster Books, 1667
shipwreck, 1120, 1694, 1744, 1811, 1859, 1909, 1910, 1912, 1915, 1919
Mary Rose, 1545
Sidney Street Siege, 1911
silk, 1717
Singapore, 1819
slavery, 1441, 1606, 1652, 1672, 1699, 1713, 1772, 1781, 1788, 1807, 1812, 1833, 1837, 1862
Slave Trade Act, 1799
Sligo, 1749
smallpox, *see* disease
smuggler, 1735
South Africa, 1660, 1867

Spain, 1581, 1975
spa towns, 1626
Speenhamland, 1795
Spinning Wheel Premium Entitlement List, 1796
Spiritualism, 1848
Society of Genealogists, 1911
Society for Promoting Christian Knowledge, 1698
Somerset, 1912, 1942
South Africa, 1498, 1652, 1660, 1795, 1806, 1836, 1867, 1877, 1886, 1910, 1931, 1934, 1948, 1961
Southampton, 1630
South Sea Bubble, 1720
spa town, 1626
Special Air Service, 1941
Speed, John, 1611
Spinning Jenny, 1764
Stamp Act, 1710
Stamp Duty Act, 1783
Status of Children Born Abroad Act, 1350
Statute of:
  Artificers, 1558
  Cambridge, 1388
  Labourers, 1351, 1450
  Mortmain, 1279
  Quia Emptores, 1290
  Quo Warranto, 1290
  Westminster, 1285
  Wills, 1540
  Winchester, 1285
steam engine, 1775
Stent Records of Inverkeithing, The, 1634
Stepney, 1870
still birth, 1926, 1960
St Kitts, 1622
Stopes, Marie, 1921
storm, 1286–7, 1658, 1694, 1703, 1811, 1859, 1866, 1871, 1874, 1987
Stowmarket, 1871
Stuart, Arbella, 1615
Sudan, 1868
Suez Canal, 1868
Suffragette, 1903, 1911, 1913
Sugar and Molasses Act, 1733
Sunderland, 1831, 1883
Supplementary Militia Act, 1796
surnames, 1067, 1130, 1187, 1400s, 1465
Surrey, 1709
Sutherland, 1735
Swansea, 1941

synagogue register, 1670
syphilis, 1495

Tasmania, 1803, 1856
Taunton, 1685
Taxatio Ecclesiastica, 1288
taxation, 1086, 1161, 1288, 1290, 1341,
    1523, 1525, 1597, 1642, 1660, 1661,
    1695, 1698, 1710, 1747, 1777, 1783, 1851,
    1894, 1975, 1990, 1991
    beard, 1535
    female servants, 1785
    game and horses, 1784
    hair powder and death duty, 1795
    hearth, 1662, 1696
    income, 1798
    inheritance, 1906
    land, 1693
    poll, 1377, 1379, 1381, 1660, 1694, 1695,
      1990, 1991
    sheep, 1549
    ship, 1634
    silver plate, 1756
    window, 1696, 1766, 1784
Tay Bridge disaster, 1879
telegraph, 1896
telescope, 1680
television, 1925
Temperance societies, 1820s
Tenures Abolition Act, 1660
Test Act, 1673
Test and Corporation Act, 1828
theatre, 1838
threshing machine, 1784
tithe, 1188
    Applotment Books, 1823
    Commutation Act, 1836
Toleration Act, 1689
Toll-books, 1555
Tolpuddle Martyrs, 1834
Topographical Dictionary of England, 1831
    Ireland, 1837
    Scotland, 1846
    Wales, 1833
Tower of London, 1244, 1615
trade unions, 1799, 1824, 1871
tram, horse-drawn, 1870
transportation (punishment), 1615, 1718,
    1779, 1803, 1868
Transvaal, 1877, 1879, 1886, 1910
Trinity House, 1514
turnpike, 1663
Turpin, Dick, 1738
Tyrone, County, 1740

Ulster, 1642, 1796, 1820s
    Muster Rolls of, 1630
    Plantation, 1606
Union, Act of, 1707, 1800
Union of Scotland and England, 1603
United States, 1776, 1783, 1790, 1803,
    1815, 1823, 1829, 1850, 1945, 1947,
    1963, 1968
universities, *see* education
Utrecht, Treaty of, 1713

Vagabonds Act, 1495, 1547, 1572, 1598
Valor Ecclesiasticus, 1535
Van Diemen's Land, *see* Tasmania
Victoria County History, 1899
Virginia, 1618

Wakefield, 1704
Wales, 1188, 1277, 1283, 1288, 1347,
    1400s, 1516, 1535, 1536, 1538, 1540,
    1542, 1562, 1573, 1579, 1582, 1600,
    1611, 1653, 1675, 1696, 1778, 1800,
    1833, 1835, 1838, 1839, 1846, 1851,1865,
    1867, 1870, 1888, 1891, 1898, 1913,
    1967, 1969, 1972, 1974, 1976, 1999,
    2013–14
war, 1639, 1778, 1793, 1803
    American Civil War, 1861
    American War of Independence, 1775
    Anglo,Afghan, 1841
    Anglo-Boer, 1880, 1899
    Anglo-Dutch, 1652, 1664, 1672, 1674
    Anglo-Spanish, 1585, 1654
    Cold, 1947
    Crimean, 1854
    Falklands, 1982
    Franco, Prussian, 1870
    French Revolution, 1789
    Greek War of Independence, 1821
    Gulf War (first), 1990
    Gulf War (second), 2003
    Hundred Years, 1337
    Korean, 1951
    Napoleonic, 1803
    Nine Years, 1595
    Opium, 1839
    Roses, of the, 1455
    Scottish Independence, 1296
    Seven Years, 1756
    Spanish Civil, 1937
    Thirty Years, 1618
    World War, First , 1914, 2011
    World War, Second, 1939, 1973